Maths Out Loud
Year 5

by
Fran Mosley

Acknowledgements

Jane Prothero and Woodlands Primary School, Leeds

Karen Holman and Paddox Primary School, Rugby

Heather Nixon and Gayhurst Primary School, Buckinghamshire

John Ellard and Kingsley Primary School, Northampton

Jackie Smith, Catherine Torr and Roberttown CE J & I School, Kirklees

Wendy Price and St Martin's CE Primary School, Wolverhampton

Helen Elis Jones, University of Wales, Bangor

Ruth Trundley, Devon Curriculum Services, Exeter

Trudy Lines and Bibury CE Primary School, Gloucestershire

Elaine Folen and St Paul's Infant School, Surrey

Jane Airey and Frith Manor Primary School, Barnet

Beverley Godfrey, South Wales Home Educators' Network

Kay Brunsdon and Gwyrosydd Infant School, Swansea

Keith Cadman, Wolverhampton Advisory Services

Helen Andrews and Blue Coat School, Birmingham

Oakridge Parochial School, Gloucestershire

The Islington BEAM Development Group

Published by BEAM Education

Maze Workshops

72a Southgate Road

London N1 3JT

Telephone 020 7684 3323

Fax 020 7684 3334

Email info@beam.co.uk

www.beam.co.uk

© Beam Education 2006

All rights reserved. None of the material in this
book may be reproduced in any form without prior
permission of the publisher

ISBN 1 903142 87 3

British Library Cataloguing-in-Publication Data

Data available

Edited by Ros Elphinstone and Marion Dill

Designed by Malena Wilson-Max

Photographs by Len Cross

Thanks to Rotherfield Primary School

Printed in England by Cromwell Press Ltd

Contents

Introduction

Language plays an important part in the learning of mathematics – especially oral language. Children's relationship to the subject, their grasp of it and sense of ownership all depend on discussion and interaction – as do the social relationships that provide the context for learning. A classroom where children talk about mathematics is one that will help build their confidence and transform their whole attitude to learning.

Why is speaking and listening important in maths?

- Talking is creative. In expressing thoughts and discussing ideas, children actually shape these ideas, make connections and hone their definitions of what words mean.
- You cannot teach what a word means – you can only introduce it, explain it, then let children try it out, misuse it, see when it works and how it fits with what they already know and, eventually, make it their own.
- Speaking and listening to other children involves and motivates children – they are more likely to learn and remember than when engaging silently with a textbook or worksheet.
- As you listen to children, you identify children's misconceptions and realise which connections (between bits of maths) they have not yet made.

How does this book help me include 'speaking and listening' in maths?

- The lessons are structured to use and develop oral language skills in mathematics. Each lesson uses one or more classroom techniques that foster the use of spoken language and listening skills.
- The grid on p17 shows those speaking and listening objectives that are suitable for developing through the medium of mathematics. Each lesson addresses one of these objectives.
- The lessons draw on a bank of classroom techniques which are described on p8. These techniques are designed to promote children's use of speaking and listening in a variety of ways.

How does 'using and applying mathematics' fit in with these lessons?

- Many of the mathematical activities in this book involve problem solving, communication and reasoning, all key areas of 'using and applying mathematics' (U&A). Where this aspect of a lesson is particularly significant, this is acknowledged and expanded on in one of the 'asides' to the main lesson.

What about children with particular needs?

- For children who have impaired hearing, communication is particularly important, as it is all too easy for them to become isolated from their peers. Speaking and listening activities, even if adapted, simplified or supported by an assistant, help such children be a part of their learning community and to participate in the curriculum on offer.

- Children who speak English as an additional language benefit from speaking and listening activities, especially where these are accompanied by diagrams, drawings or the manipulation of numbers or shapes, which help give meaning to the language. Check that they understand the key words needed for the topic being discussed and, where possible, model the activity, paying particular attention to the use of these key words. Remember to build in time for thinking and reflecting on oral work.

- Differences in children's backgrounds affect the way they speak to their peers and adults. The lessons in this book can help children acquire a rich repertoire of ways to interact and work with others. Children who are less confident with written forms can develop confidence through speaking and listening.

- Gender can be an issue in acquiring and using speaking and listening skills. Girls may be collaborative and tentative, while boys sometimes can be more assertive about expressing their ideas. Address such differences by planning different groups, partners, classroom seating and activities. These lessons build on children's strengths and challenge them in areas where they are less strong.

What are the 'personal skills' learning objectives?

- There is a range of personal and social skills that children need to develop across the curriculum and throughout their school career. These include enquiry skills, creative thinking skills and ways of working with others. Some are particularly relevant to the maths classroom, and these are listed on the grid on p18.

What about assessment?

- Each lesson concludes with a section called 'Assessment for learning', which offers suggestions for what to look out for during the lesson and questions to ask in order to assess children's learning of all three learning objectives. There is also help on what may lie behind children's failure to meet these objectives and suggestions for teaching that might rectify the situation.

- Each section of four lessons includes a sheet of self-assessment statements to be printed from the accompanying CD-ROM and to be filled in at the end of each lesson or when all four are completed. Display the sheet and also give children their own copies. Then go through the statements, discussing and interpreting them as necessary. Ask children to complete their self-assessments with a partner they frequently work with. They should each fill in their own sheet, then look at it with their partner who adds their own viewpoint.

How can I make the best use of these lessons?

- Aim to develop a supportive classroom climate, where all ideas are accepted and considered, even if they may seem strange or incorrect. You will need to model this yourself in order for children to see what acceptance and open-mindedness look like.
- Create an ethos of challenge, where children are required to think about puzzles and questions.
- Slow down. Don't expect answers straight away when you ask questions. Build in thinking time where you do not communicate with the children, so that they have to reflect on their answers before making them. Expect quality rather than quantity.
- Model the language of discussion. Children who may be used to maths being either 'correct' or 'incorrect' need to learn by example what debate means. Choose a debating partner from the class, or work with another adult, and demonstrate uncertainty, challenge, exploration, questioning ...
- Tell children what they will be learning in the lesson. Each lesson concludes with an 'Assessment for learning' section offering suggestions for what to look out for to assess children's learning of all three learning objectives. Share these with the children at the start of the lesson to involve them in their own learning process.

How should I get the best out of different groupings?

- Get children used to working in a range of different groupings: pairs, threes or fours or as a whole class.
- Organise pairs in different ways on different occasions: familiar maths partners (who can communicate well); pairs of friends (who enjoy working together); children of differing abilities (who can learn something from each other); someone they don't know (to get them used to talking and listening respectfully to any other person).
- Give children working in pairs and groups some time for independent thought and work.
- Support pairs when they prepare to report back to the class. Go over with them what they have done or discovered and what they might say about this. Help them make brief notes – just single words or phrases – to remind them what they are going to say. If you are busy, ask an assistant or another child to take over your role. Then, when it comes to feedback time, support them by gentle probes or questions: "What did you do next?" or "What do your notes say?"

Classroom techniques used in this book

Ways of working

Peer tutoring
pairs of children

good for

This technique can benefit both the child who is being 'taught' and also the 'tutor' who develops a clearer understanding of what they themselves have learned and, in explaining it, can make new connections and solidify old ones. Children often make the best teachers, because they are close to the state of not knowing and can remember what helped them bridge the gap towards understanding.

how to organise it

'Peer tutoring' can work informally – children work in mixed ability pairs, and if one child understands an aspect of the work that the other doesn't, they work together in a tutor/pupil relationship to make sure the understanding is shared by both. Alternatively, you can structure it more formally. Observe children at work and identify those who are confident and accurate with the current piece of mathematics. Give them the title of 'Expert' and ask them to work with individuals needing support. Don't overuse this: the tutor has a right to work and learn at their own level, and tutoring others should only play a small part in their school lives.

Talking partners
pairs of children

good for

This technique helps children develop and practise the skills of collaboration in an unstructured way. Children can articulate their thinking, listen to one another and support each other's learning in a 'safe' situation.

how to organise it

Pairs who have previously worked together (for example, 'One between two', below) work together informally. The children in these pairs have had time to build up trust between them, and should have the confidence to tackle a new, less structured task. If you regularly use 'Talking partners', pairs of children will get used to working together. This helps them develop confidence, but runs the risk that children mutually reinforce their misunderstandings. In this case, changing partners occasionally can bring fresh life to the class by creating new meetings of minds.

One between two
pairs of children

good for

This technique helps children develop their skills of explaining, questioning and listening – behaviours that are linked to positive learning outcomes. Use it when the children have two or more problems or calculations to solve.

how to organise it

Pairs share a pencil (or calculator or other tool), and each assumes one of two roles: 'Solver' or 'Recorder'. (Supplying just one pencil encourages children to stay in role by preventing the Solver from making their own notes.)

The Solver has a problem and works through it out loud. The Recorder keeps a written record of what the Solver is doing. If the Solver needs something written down or a calculation done on the calculator, they must ask the Recorder to do this for them. If the Recorder is not sure of what the Solver is doing, they ask for further explanations, but do not engage in actually solving the problem. After each problem, children swap roles.

Introduce this way of working by modelling it yourself with a confident child partner: you talk through your own method of solving a problem, and the child records this thought process on the board.

Barrier games/Telephone conversations

pairs of children

good for

These techniques help children focus on spoken language rather than gesture or facial expression. The children must listen carefully to what is said, because they cannot see the person speaking.

how to organise it

Barrier games focus on giving and receiving instructions. Pairs of children work with a book or screen between them, so that they cannot see each other's work. The speaker gives information or instructions to the listener. The listener, in turn, asks questions to clarify understanding and gain information.

In 'Telephone conversations', the technique is taken further, as children sit back to back, with only imaginary 'telephones' for conversation.

Rotating roles

groups of various sizes

good for

Working in a small group to solve a problem encourages children to articulate their thinking and support each other's learning.

how to organise it

Careful structuring discourages individuals from taking the lead too often. Assign different roles to the children in the group: Chairperson, Reader, Recorder, Questioner, and so on. Over time, everyone has a turn at each role. You may wish to give children 'role labels' to remind them of their current role.

When you introduce this technique, model the role of chairperson in a group, with the rest of the class watching. Show how to include everyone and then discuss with the children what you have done, so as to make explicit techniques that they can use.

Discussion

Think, pair, share
groups of four

good for

Putting pairs together to work as a group of four helps avoid the situation where children in pairs mutually reinforce their common misunderstandings. It gives children time to think on their own, rehearse their thoughts with a partner and then discuss in a larger group. This encourages everyone to join in and discourages the 'quick thinkers' from dominating a discussion.

how to organise it

The technique is a development of 'Tell your partner' and involves the following:
- One or two minutes for individuals to think about a problem or statement and, possibly, to jot down their initial thoughts
- Two or three minutes where individuals work in pairs to share their thoughts
- Four or five minutes for two pairs to join together and discuss
- If you wish, you can also allow ten minutes for reporting back from some or all groups and whole-class discussion.

You can vary this pattern and the timings, but always aim to give children some 'private' thinking time.

Talking stick
any number of children

good for

Giving all children a turn at speaking and being listened to.

how to organise it

Provide the class with decorated sticks, which confer status on whoever holds them. Then, in a small or large group (or even the whole class), make it the rule that only the person holding the stick may speak, while the other children listen. You can use the stick in various ways: pass it around the circle; tell the child with the stick to pass it to whoever they want to speak next; have a chairperson who decides who will hold the stick next; ask the person with the stick to repeat what the previous person said before adding their own comments or ideas.

Tell your partner
pairs

good for

Whole-class question-and-answer sessions favour the quick and the confident and do not provide time and space for slower thinkers. This technique involves all children in answering questions and in discussion.

how to organise it

Do this in one of two ways:

- When you have just asked a question or presented an idea to think about, ask each child to turn to their neighbour or partner and tell them the answer. They then take turns to speak and to listen.
- Work less formally, simply asking children to talk over their ideas with a partner. Children may find this sharing difficult at first. They may not value talking to another child, preferring to talk to the teacher or not expressing their ideas at all. In this case, do some work on listening skills such as timing 'a minute each way' or repeating back to their partner what they have just said.

Devil's advocate

any number of children

good for

Statements – false or ambiguous as well as true – are often better than questions at provoking discussion.

how to organise it

In discussion with children, take the role of 'Devil's advocate', in which you make statements for them to agree or disagree with and to argue about.

To avoid confusing children by making false statements yourself, mention 'a friend' or 'someone you know' who makes these statements (a version of the 'silly teddy' who, in Nursery and Reception, makes mistakes for the children to correct). Alternatively, explain that when you make statements with your hands behind your back, your fingers may be crossed and you may be saying things that are not true.

Reporting back

Ticket to explain

Individuals

good for

This is a way of structuring feedback which helps children get the maximum out of offering explanations to the class. Everyone hears a method explained twice, and children have to listen carefully to their peers, rather than simply think about their own method.

how to organise it

When individuals want to explain their method of working to the class, their 'ticket' to be able to do this is to re-explain the method demonstrated by the child immediately before them. Or children work with a partner and explain their ideas to each other. When called on to speak, they explain their partner's idea and then their own.

Heads or tails
pairs of children

good for

When pairs of children work together, one child may rely heavily on the other to make decisions and to communicate or one child may take over, despite the efforts of the other child to have a say. This technique encourages pairs to work together to understand something and helps prevent an uneven workload.

how to organise it

Invite pairs to the front of the class to explain their ideas or solutions. When they get to the front, ask them to nominate who is heads and who is tails, then toss a coin to decide which of them does the talking. They have one opportunity to 'ask a friend' (probably their partner). As all children in the class know that they may be chosen to speak in this way, because the toss of the coin could make either of them into the 'explainer', they are motivated to work with their partner to reach a common understanding. Assigning the choice of explainer to the toss of a coin stops children feeling that anyone is picking on them personally (do warn them in advance, though!). Variation: If a pair of children has different ideas on a topic, ask both to offer explanations of each other's ideas.

1, 2, 3, 4
groups of four

good for

This technique offers the same benefits as 'Heads or tails', but is used for groups of four children rather than pairs.

how to organise it

This is a technique identical to 'Heads or tails', but with groups of four. Instead of tossing a coin, children are numbered 1 to 4, and the speaker is chosen by the roll of a dice (if 5 or 6 come up, simply roll again).

Additional techniques

Below are some further classroom techniques that are referred to in the lessons in this book.

Ideas map
whole class

good for

This technique enables children to identify what they know and what they don't know and so equips them to monitor their own learning.

Drawing up an ideas map at the start of teaching a topic can produce valuable material on which to base initial assessments of the children's understanding. It also serves to steer the children towards what they will be learning. Return to the map and even revise and adapt it after a period of teaching in order to consolidate children's learning.

how to organise it

Develop your first ideas maps as a whole class. Hold a creative brainstorm with the children to conjure up as many terms connected to a topic as they can think of, with you adding more terms as appropriate – scribe the contributions and, as you do so, prompt the children to help you establish connections between them.

Once children are used to the idea, they can work in groups or as individuals to draw up ideas maps of their own. They can either work from scratch or you can start them off with a whole-class creative brainstorm, where you collect terms but don't make any connections. Children then devise their own ideas map, using some or all of these terms.

When they construct the map, children aim to link terms together and write on the links something to describe the nature of the connection. Some teachers ask children to write individual words or phrases on sticky notes, so that they can move them around and explore different links before settling on the ones they want to describe.

Ideas board
whole class

good for

An ideas board is a place where children display their work to the rest of the class informally and quickly. It also provides a useful place for you to record ideas and problems that you want children to think about.

how to organise it

The visual aspect of display is not a priority with an ideas board – it is more like a notice board where ideas and information can be shared. Make sure you remove items regularly to keep it fresh and up to date.

Chewing the fat
any number of children

good for

Leaving ideas or questions unresolved provides thoughtful children with the opportunity to extend their thinking and can help develop good habits. Many real mathematicians like to have problems to think about in odd moments, just as some people like crossword clues or chess moves to occupy their mind.

how to organise it

Sometimes end a lesson with ideas, problems or challenges for children to ponder in their own time as you may have run out of time or one of the children has come up with a question or an idea which can only be discussed the next day.

Reframing

any number of children

good for

'Reframing' alters the meaning of something by altering its context or description. It helps children find their way into a difficult or new idea by hearing it rephrased and enlarged.

how to organise it

Rephrase children's words using a variety of language: "You read that out as 'twenty-five multiplied by seven'. That means seven lots of 25." After a few seconds, say: "Imagine a pile of 25 beans, and you've got seven piles like that."

Goldfish bowl

whole class

good for

This technique enables you to demonstrate a new game or activity to any number of children in a practical and accessible way and to deal with children's queries and misunderstandings as they arise.

how to organise it

Ask the class to stand or sit in a circle around one pair or group of children and to watch as they follow your instructions to demonstrate a game or activity. You can adapt this technique in various ways. For example, children who want to suggest a move to a player can stand behind them and put a hand on their shoulder to indicate that they have a suggestion to make. Alternatively, you can stop the game at any time and discuss with the observers what is happening, asking for their comments and suggestions.

Charts

Classroom techniques

This chart shows which of the classroom techniques previously described are used in which lessons.

	NUMBERS AND THE NUMBER SYSTEM	FRACTIONS, DECIMALS, PERCENTAGES, RATIO AND PROPORTION	ADDITION AND SUBTRACTION	MULTIPLICATION AND DIVISION	HANDLING DATA	MEASURES	SHAPE AND SPACE
	Lesson	Lesson	Lesson	Lesson	Lesson	Lesson	Lesson
One between two	1		10				25
Talking partners		6	12	13	17		28
Rotating roles	3	7					27
Peer tutoring	2		9				
Barrier games / Telephone conversations					19	21	
Tell your partner					18		26
Devil's advocate		5		16			
Think, pair, share				14	20	23	
Ticket to explain						24	
Heads or tails / 1, 2, 3, 4	4	8	11	15		22	

Speaking and listening skills

This chart shows which speaking and listening skills are practised in which lessons.

	NUMBERS AND THE NUMBER SYSTEM	FRACTIONS, DECIMALS, PERCENTAGES, RATIO AND PROPORTION	ADDITION AND SUBTRACTION	MULTIPLICATION AND DIVISION	HANDLING DATA	MEASURES	SHAPE AND SPACE
	Lesson	Lesson	Lesson	Lesson	Lesson	Lesson	Lesson
Discuss progress of work	2						
Explain and justify thinking				13, 15	18	24	26
Use precise language to explain ideas or give information	1		10			21	
Share and discuss ideas and reach consensus	4	5, 7	9	14	17		27
Reach a common understanding with a partner			11		19		25
Use the processes and language of decision making		6				22	
Contribute to small-group and whole-class discussion	3	8	12	16	20	23	28

Personal skills

This chart shows which personal skills are practised in which lessons.

	NUMBERS AND THE NUMBER SYSTEM	FRACTIONS, DECIMALS, PERCENTAGES, RATIO AND PROPORTION	ADDITION AND SUBTRACTION	MULTIPLICATION AND DIVISION	HANDLING DATA	MEASURES	SHAPE AND SPACE
	Lesson	Lesson	Lesson	Lesson	Lesson	Lesson	Lesson
Organise work							
Plan a sequence of work			12				
Plan and manage a group task							27
Use different approaches to tackle a problem	4	8	11			24	
Organise findings					20		
Work with others							
Discuss and agree ways of working	3			15			
Work cooperatively with others		7	10	14		21	
Overcome difficulties and recover from mistakes			9		17		25
Show awareness and understanding of others' needs	2						
Improve learning and performance							
Reflect on learning		6		13	18		
Critically evaluate own work	1					22	
Assess learning progress							28
Take pride in work					19		26
Develop confidence in own judgements		5		16		23	

Lessons

Word Bank.

March April May June

September October November December

Numbers and the number system

Learning objectives

	Lessons			
	1	**2**	**3**	**4**
ⓜ Maths objectives				
recognise and extend number sequences	●			
read and write whole numbers to a million		●		
find pairs of factors for any number to 100			●	
find the difference between two four-digit numbers				●
Speaking and listening skills				
use precise language to explain ideas or give information	●			
discuss progress of work		●		
contribute to small-group discussion			●	
share and discuss ideas and reach consensus				●
Personal skills				
improve learning and performance: critically evaluate own work	●			
work with others: show awareness and understanding of others' needs		●		
work with others: discuss and agree ways of working			●	
organise work: use different approaches to tackle a problem				●

About these lessons

Lesson 1: Calculator number sequences

 Recognise and extend number sequences

Working with number sequences helps children see that pattern and regularity are important features of mathematics. In this activity, children create number sequences, identify patterns and predict further numbers in a sequence.

 Use precise language to explain ideas or give information

Classroom technique: One between two

The activity is structured so that children must talk about their work. They make verbal predictions about the next number that the calculator will show and discuss and agree descriptions of the number patterns produced. The teacher's questions ask children to justify their choice of sequence and their explanation of the patterns.

 Improve learning and performance: critically evaluate own work

It is important that children have a reasonable sense of how well they are achieving the set goals and of how they are approaching their work. Appropriate questioning and discussion in this lesson helps children focus on these questions.

Lesson 2: Numbers to a million

 Read and write whole numbers to a million

Learning to read and write large numbers may seem straightforward to adults. For children to develop competence in this area, they need to practise their skills. This activity gives them such practice in a structured and supportive context.

 Discuss progress of work

Classroom technique: Peer tutoring

Children work in a small group, sharing the responsibility for learning. If one child understands an aspect of the work and another doesn't, the group works together to make sure that the understanding is shared by all. Sharing the responsibility in this way means children must discuss their achievement and progress in the task in order to decide whether peer tutoring is necessary and how this will be undertaken.

 Work with others: show awareness and understanding of others' needs

Children need to consider the needs of other people to function well as a group. This might include speaking clearly or pacing the giving of information. In addition, children acting as peer tutors must think about what their 'pupil' needs to help them understand the mathematics.

Lesson 3: Factor pairs

 Find pairs of factors for any number to 100

In this lesson, children explore factor pairs using tiles or squared paper and calculators. This models the ways that multiples are made up from factors, which provides a solid basis for understanding the relevant concepts.

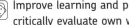 **Contribute to small-group discussion**

Classroom technique: Rotating roles

Each child has a different role to play and, during the activity, has the opportunity to fulfil all three roles. This means that all children have the full range of experience provided by the activity. Because each role is dependent on each other role, the children need to discuss and negotiate a common purpose and understanding.

 Work with others: discuss and agree ways of working

Working in a group of three, children must cooperate, discuss and reach agreement in order to fulfil the task they have been set.

Lesson 4: Finding differences

 Find the difference between two four-digit numbers

The puzzle in this activity requires children to apply both their knowledge of place value and a range of thinking skills. They are unlikely to come up with a general solution that fits all cases, but can be expected to develop and explain some general strategies.

 Share and discuss ideas and reach consensus

Classroom technique: Heads or tails

Pairs know that if they are invited to the front of the class to explain their ideas or solutions, one of them must do the talking – but they don't know in advance which of them it will be (this is decided by the toss of a coin). This means pairs must collaborate, share their ideas, agree solutions and take shared responsibility for understanding these solutions.

Organise work: use different approaches to tackle a problem

Pairs share a challenge, materials and tools. They must agree together, verbally or non-verbally, how to approach the task, share decision making and reach a conclusion.

Calculator number sequences
Classroom technique: One between two

Learning objectives

m **Maths**
Recognise and extend number sequences

Speaking and listening
'Explain what you think and why you think it'
Use precise language to explain ideas or give information

Personal skills
'Evaluate your own work'
Improve learning and performance: critically evaluate own work

W **Words and phrases**
add, subtract, minus, rule, pattern, sequence, operation, positive, negative, generate

r **Resources**
number fans
display copy of RS1
for each pair:
copy of RS1 (optional)
calculator

Modelling
Model ways of talking about sequences for children to make use of in the main activity.

The constant function
Show the children, if necessary, how to use the calculator to carry out an operation such as '+5' repeatedly. (On many calculators pressing '5 + = = =' displays 5 10 15 20...) Key in the operation, then start the sequence at any number. (Pressing '5 + = 9 = = = =' should give 9 14 19 24 29.)

One between two
Sharing a calculator and a common task helps children focus on working collaboratively.

U&A Searching for pattern in results
Children look for and describe the patterns in their results, then use these to predict further numbers in the sequence.
Starting number: 99
Operation: '+15'
99 114 129 144 159
174 189 204 219 234
249
"The units keep going 9 4 9 4. The other numbers go like this: 9 gap 11 12 gap 14 15 gap..."

Introduction

Write up an operation such as '+9'. Use a calculator to generate the sequence, starting at 0. Children work in pairs. Ask the pairs to predict the next number in the sequence each time and to show their prediction, using a number fan.

m *Will I ever get a 5 in the units place? Why do you think that?*

Tell your partner how you work out the next number each time.

Pairs

Display RS1 on the board or give each pair of children a copy of RS1. Children agree an operation and a starting number, which they write down on a blank sheet of paper. They then key the operation into the calculator using the constant function.

Child A is in charge of the calculator and uses it to generate the sequence.

Starting number	Operation	Sequence
20	+15	20 35 50 65 80 95 110 125

Child B predicts the next number that will appear each time. Child A says whether or not they agree with this prediction before pressing the '=' key to find out if they are right.

Child B writes down the numbers produced on blank paper.

After they have created a sequence of 10 numbers, the children swap roles.

m *Will you get any negative numbers in your sequence? How do you know?*

m *Explain the number pattern you are getting.*

Tell your partner what you think is happening in this sequence.

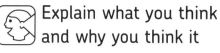
Tell me why you chose that operation and starting number.

How do you think you are doing at predicting the sequences?

Which sequence do you think you had to work hardest at?

Questioning

Encourage children to reflect on which aspects of the work they find easy or hard and on how well they are challenging themselves.

Support: Write up the sequence of keys to press, including the operation and starting point.

Extend: Children generate their own rules and choose their own starting points (ask them to record these for you). They also explore the operation 'x2'.

Plenary

Generate your own sequence, without telling the class your rule. Pairs discuss together what your rule must be, and why they think that.

Ask a few pairs for suggestions and reasons.

Also ask for descriptions of the number pattern.

How do you know the rule is not about dividing?

Tell the class whether the rule could be multiplying. How do you know?

Assessment for learning

Can the children

Predict the number sequence produced by repeatedly adding 1.5? By repeatedly subtracting 9?

Explain how to work out the next number in the sequence?

If not

Practise counting in jumps of various sizes with the class, modelling the jumps on a number line if appropriate.

Ask another child to offer this explanation and invite the first child to repeat what they have said. Model how to write out the numbers that show the repeating pattern and how to use these to work out the next number in the sequence.

10	13	16	19	22	25	28
31	34	37	40	43		

Check their work for errors and for ways they can improve it?

Ask for a selection of impressive work to display around the school and encourage children to polish up and present one of their sequences for this purpose.

Numbers to a million

Classroom technique: Peer tutoring

Learning objectives

(m) **Maths**
Read and write whole numbers to a million

(≋) **Speaking and listening**
'Talk about the progress of your work'
Discuss progress of work

(☺) **Personal skills**
'Show that you understand what other people need'
Work with others: show awareness and understanding of others' needs

(W) **Words and phrases**
units, ones, tens, hundreds, thousands, ten thousand, hundred thousand, million, digit

(r) **Resources**
for each group:
digit cards cut from RS2
role labels cut from RS3 (optional)
calculator

Reading numbers

5 'five'
45 'forty-five'
745 'seven hundred and forty-five'

Remind children about the convention of leaving a space before each cluster of three digits: 2 234 745.

Peer tutoring

The group record the numbers they make and also any problems that arise. They work on these difficulties as a group, aiming for all members of the group to understand how to read and record the numbers made.

Pattern

If children don't do so themselves, point out how the pattern of HTO repeats in the thousands: HTh TTh Th. This means the three digits to the right of the hundreds can be read like any HTO number, with the word 'thousands' added.

Introduction

Write up a single-digit number and then repeatedly write digits to the left of it. Ask the class to read out each new number as it is made.

(m) *What is the value of the digit 7? And if I put another 7 to the left of it, what would that 7 be worth?*

Groups of three

Give each group of three children two sets of digit cards (cut from RS2). If required, they can use role labels (cut from RS3) to remind them of their tasks.

The 'Number Maker' arranges some of the cards to make any number to a million.

The 'Reader' looks at the cards and reads out the number.

The 'Calculator Holder' listens to the Reader and keys the number into the calculator, without looking at the number cards.

The group then check their work by comparing the calculator display with the number made from the number cards.

Children rotate roles so that each child gets one or more turns in each role.

(m) *Can you read a number when it includes two zeros? Show me.*

(m) *Let's see you make a number that is more than ten thousand.*

(≋) *Which of the three roles do you find easiest? And which role do you need to practise more?*

(≋) *What difficult numbers have you come across so far? Can you say why that number is difficult to read?*

(≋) *What rules have you worked out to remember how to say the number?*

(☺) *How might you help Dave remember what the number in each position is worth?*

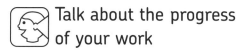
Support: Provide a labelled base board.

HTh	TTh	Th	H	T	O
4	5	7	9	0	2

Extend: Introduce a decimal point card – remind children about the conventions about using zeros to the right of the decimal point – and make seven- or eight-digit numbers.

Plenary

Read out a six-digit number to the class. One member of each group keys this into their calculator.

Now ask for one digit to be changed to another by adding or subtracting one number – for example, start with 450 923 and have this changed to 460 923.

The other two members of the group confer about the number to be added or subtracted and instruct the child with the calculator which keys to press.

(m) *How do you work out the value of the digit to be changed?*

(speech) *Tell me one thing you need to think about when you are telling the person with the calculator what to do.*

Assessment for learning

Can the children	If not
(m) Read aloud any six-digit whole number? Any seven- or eight-digit whole number? Any decimal number?	(m) Display a base board as shown above (or one adapted to show decimals). Change the numbers on it daily and ask children to read out and discuss the new number.
(speech) Identify a 'tricky' number or category of numbers?	(speech) Collect in 'tricky' numbers from the class and discuss together why they are difficult to read or write. Offer strategies for dealing with such numbers.
(face) Show patience when another group member has difficulties?	(face) Remind children that we all need people to be patient with us at times. Offer models of how to be patient with others, perhaps in a role-play situation.

Factor pairs

Classroom technique: Rotating roles

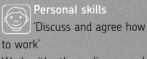
Role labels

If necessary, you can use role
labels, as in Lesson 2, to remind
children of their individual tasks.

**U&A Finding all
the factor pairs**

When children think they have
found all the factor pairs, ask
how they can check this. They
should work out that they need
to test for all possible factors in
turn, either mentally or with the
calculator or squared paper.

Introduction

Display RS4 to the class and ask for two volunteers
to help you demonstrate the main activity.

Choose a number from the circle and write it
in the box.

Child A draws a rectangle on 5-cm squared
paper or a grid on the whiteboard, containing that
many squares (for example, three rows of ten squares
if the number chosen was 30).

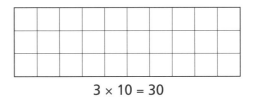

$$3 \times 10 = 30$$

Ask the child to tell you what multiplication to key into
the calculator as a check (in this case, '3 × 10 ='). Read
out the answer. As a group, briefly discuss what the
factor pair is.

Child B records this factor pair on RS4.

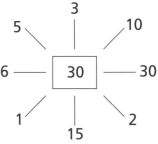

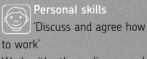 *What rectangle can you draw that will have 12
squares? Would any other rectangles work?*

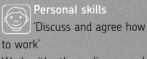 *How can we check that we have found them all?*

Groups of three

Give each group of three a calculator and some
squared paper. Children choose a number and do the
same activity. They record by drawing their own
diagram. After each calculation they rotate roles and
continue, adding as many extra lines as necessary.

When they think they have found all the factor pairs,
they start working with a new number.

(m) *What factor might you try first? Why that one?*

(m) *You know 4 is a factor of that number, so what else must be a factor? How do you know that?*

(m) *How do you use the calculator to check for factors of that number?*

Factors of 80		
Number tried	Does it work?	Factor pair
1	yes	1, 80
2	yes	2, 40
3	no	
4	yes	4, 20
5	yes	5, 16
6	no	
7	no	
8	yes	8, 10
9	no	
10	yes	10, 8
11	no	
12	no	
13	no	
14	no	

(☺) *Try to explain that idea to your group, so they all understand what you mean.*

(☺) *Who decides when you have found all the factors? Are you sharing the decision making?*

Support: Work with 12 or 24 and use square tiles that can be moved around easily.

Extend: Children find their own number to work with – one that is 'rich in factors' – by multiplying together several small numbers.

Plenary

Choose a number such as 80, 100, 72 or 60. Collect and record all factor pairs on the board, demonstrating what you mean by systematic recording.

Invite individuals to talk about the method(s) they found earlier for checking they had found all possible factor pairs of a number.

(☺) *Explain to the class how you can tell from the calculator display that 7 is not a factor of 100.*

Assessment for learning

Can the children

(m) Find all the factor pairs for 12, 20, 48?

(☺) Explain an idea to the rest of the group?

(☺) Take on a new role with good grace, as required by the activity?

If not

(m) Focus on developing the skill of being systematic. Look for ways to focus on this in other mathematical contexts.

(☺) Help improve children's vocabulary – and, consequently, their confidence – through frequent discussions involving factors and multiples.

(☺) Consider providing more support for children who lack the confidence to fulfil a particular role or try putting them in a different group.

Finding differences

Classroom technique: Heads or tails

Learning objectives

(m) Maths
Find the difference between two four-digit numbers

(👤) Speaking and listening
'Share ideas and reach an agreement with your partner'
Share and discuss ideas and reach consensus

(😊) Personal skills
'Try different ways to tackle a problem'
Organise work: use different approaches to tackle a problem

(W) Words and phrases
digit, difference, subtract, order, position, place, solution, explain

(r) Resources
for each pair:
digit cards cut from RS2

Finding the difference
2 9 1 6 and 3 2 8 2
Do a written subtraction.
Make 2916 up to 3000 and add on 282.
Draw jumps on an empty number line.

Introduction

Write up two four-digit numbers and discuss different ways of finding the difference. Talk about methods (but don't do the actual calculations) before opening out the discussion to the class.

Establish the difference using one or more of the suggested methods.

(m) *Think to yourself how to find the difference between these numbers. Then I'll ask for suggestions.*

(m) *For these two numbers, which method works best?*

(👤) *How would you check your calculation? Tell your partner what you think, and why.*

Pairs

Give each pair of children a set of digit cards cut from RS2. Each child takes four cards and lays them face down in front of them.

Children turn the cards over one at a time and use them in that order to make four-digit numbers. They then read out their numbers to their partner and agree which of the two numbers is larger. Each pair combines their cards and uses them to make a pair of four-digit numbers with the smallest differences.

Ask the pairs to repeat this several times.

Pairs then agree some rules about how to rearrange the digits to get the closest pair of numbers they can.

(m) *Have you tried other ways to arrange those digits into numbers? Which way worked best?*

(m) *When two numbers are close together, what is the best way of finding the difference between them?*

(👤) *Explain to Fatima why you want to put the 8 there.*

Explanations
Listen closely to these explanations as they will give you insights into children's understanding of place value. Note teaching points for another lesson.

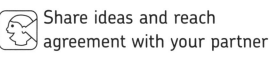
 You've tried one way of getting a small difference. What else could you try?

Support: Keep to three-digit numbers initially, moving on to four-digit numbers. An available adult helps children prepare what to say if they are chosen to speak in the plenary.

Extend: Ask for some kind of generalisation about how to place the digits, in either written or diagrammatic form.

Plenary

Heads or tails

Tell children early in the lesson that you will be using 'Heads or tails' and remind them to prepare together what they will say if they are chosen.

Give the talker one opportunity to 'phone a friend' (that is, to consult their partner) if they get stuck during their explanation.

Collect and record some of the children's numbers on the board. Pairs explain how they decided to rearrange their digit cards to make two numbers close in size, using the 'Heads or tails' technique (p12).

Now repeat the process, using more cards, to make five- or six-digit numbers.

Does anyone disagree with what Sean has said? Tell us why.

Once you've made two new numbers and found the difference, are you sure that is the smallest difference?

Assessment for learning

Can the children

Arrange eight digits to make four-digit numbers and find the difference between these?

Talk to the class about a general rule or strategy they have developed?

Show persistence in working on the problem?

If not

Revise the notion of difference. The number line offers a good model in which difference can be seen as the size of jump needed to get from one number to another.

Children may be 'taking a back seat' and allowing their partner to drive the work. Use the classroom technique 'One between two' (p8), which engineers taking of responsibilities equally.

Number games motivate children who lack confidence to keep trying at something. Make sure that adult support is provided wherever possible and that any evidence of persistence is duly acknowledged.

Self and peer assessment

Lesson 1: Calculator number sequences	I think	My partner thinks
(m) I can start at ☐ and add ☐ repeatedly and predict the numbers I will get.		
I can explain why I won't ever get 5 in the units place if I keep subtracting 2 from 100.		
I check my work for errors and try to improve it.		

Lesson 2: Numbers to a million	I think	My partner thinks
(m) I can read these numbers aloud: 478 034 50 520 24 567		
I can say what my group finds easy and difficult.		
I am patient when other people seem slower to understand than I am.		

Name _____

Lesson 3: Factor pairs	I think	My partner thinks
(m) I can find all the factor pairs for these numbers: 12, 20, 48		
I listen without interrupting when someone in my group is explaining an idea.		
I try hard at whatever role I have in my group.		

Lesson 4: Finding differences	I think	My partner thinks
(m) I can put these numbers in order: 8902 9802		
I talk to the class about what I have discovered while doing this activity.		
I see if I can find a way of getting a better solution to a problem.		

Self and peer assessment

Word Bank

March   April   May   June

September   October   November   December

Fractions, decimals, percentages, ratio and proportion

Learning objectives

	Lessons			
	5	**6**	**7**	**8**
ⓜ Maths objectives				
refine ideas about how fractions, decimals and percentages work	●			
relate fractions to their percentage representations		●		
know what each digit represents in a decimal number			●	
relate fractions to division				●
Ⓢ Speaking and listening skills				
share and discuss ideas and reach consensus	●		●	
use the processes and language of decision making		●		
contribute to whole-class discussion				●
Ⓟ Personal skills				
improve learning and performance: develop confidence in own judgements	●			
improve learning and performance: reflect on learning		●		
work with others: work cooperatively with others			●	
organise work: use different approaches to tackle a problem				●

About these lessons

Lesson 5: Using fraction number words

 Refine ideas about how fractions, decimals and percentages work

This activity focuses on some of the confused ideas children may have about fractions, decimals and percentages. By discussing which statement is true, children air these confusions and have an opportunity to clear them up.

 Share and discuss ideas and reach consensus

Classroom technique: Devil's advocate

Statements – false or ambiguous as well as true – can be better than questions at provoking discussion. In this lesson, children are presented with statements that they can agree or disagree with. Working as a class, the children are given the opportunity to argue for or against a statement, aiming to reach consensus.

 Improve learning and performance: develop confidence in own judgements

Children discuss a statement which may or may not be true and hear viewpoints put forward by other children. This helps them become clearer about – and more committed to – their own judgement about the truth of the statement.

Lesson 6: Fractions and equivalent percentages

 Relate fractions to their percentage representations

Percentages facilitate comparisons by converting quantities to a common fraction 'out of 100'. For example, comparing $\frac{1}{4}$ and $\frac{2}{10}$ is simpler when they are viewed as 25% and 20%. This game gives children an opportunity to make links between fractions and percentages.

 Use the processes and language of decision making

Classroom technique: Talking partners

This game offers opportunities for children to practise working together informally – talking and making decisions together about how to make the best use of their fraction card to win the game.

 Improve learning and performance: reflect on learning

Children need to know about the learning intentions of a mathematics lesson. Appropriate questioning and discussion can help children focus on this and think about whether or not the intentions have been fulfilled.

Lesson 7: Identifying decimal numbers

 Know what each digit represents in a decimal number

As children gain information from answers to their questions, they must check each number to see whether it meets the criterion. This requires them to focus on various properties of decimal numbers.

Share and discuss ideas and reach consensus

Classroom technique: Rotating roles

Children take turns to ask questions and answer questions. The children asking questions must pool their information and ideas in order to reach agreement about the mystery number.

 Work with others: work cooperatively with others

Working in a group and sharing a task, children must cooperate as they take turns to ask and answer questions.

Lesson 8: Finding fractions

Relate fractions to division

In this open-ended exploratory activity, children derive unknown facts from known ones. Children use the familiar strategies of doubling and halving, together with simple divisions, to find a whole range of fractions of a whole number.

Contribute to whole-class discussion

Classroom technique: Heads or tails

Pairs are invited to the front of the class to explain their ideas or solutions. When they get to the front, the toss of a coin decides which of them will do the talking. This means that both children must be prepared to talk to the class and join in the discussion about their ideas.

Organise work: use different approaches to tackle a problem

It is useful to have a repertoire of calculation strategies and to know that there is usually more than one way to tackle a problem. The class shares methods for working out fractions of a whole number, and children are then encouraged to try a range of these methods as they work with their own number.

Using fraction number words

Classroom technique: Devil's advocate

Learning objectives

(m) Maths
Refine ideas about how fractions, decimals and percentages work

Speaking and listening
'Share ideas and reach agreement as a class'
Share and discuss ideas and reach consensus

Personal skills
'Develop confidence about what you think and decide'
Improve learning and performance: develop confidence in own judgements

(W) Words and phrases
decimal point, decimal place, greater than, less than, equivalent, per cent, %, percentage, fraction, numerator, denominator, proper, improper

(r) Resources
sets of three cards cut from RS5 and RS6

Reading the words
At this stage, don't revise the meanings of the words. Simply check that children can read them.

Devil's advocate
By offering these as neutral statements you give children the opportunity to clarify and defend their ideas. Some children may state that a false statement is true. Leave it to other children to argue the case against it.

Repeat another person's explanation
One child repeats another's explanation. This technique is used elsewhere as a way of encouraging children to listen to each other's methods (see 'Ticket to explain', p11).

RS5 and RS6
TRUE:
Improper fractions: C
Percentages: A
Decimals: B
Size of fractions: B

Introduction
Brainstorm words connected to fractions, decimals and percentages and write these on the board.

Whole class
Select a set of three cards cut from RS5 or RS6, such as the set 'Improper fractions'. Choose three children to come to the front and give each child one of the cards.

The three children read out their statement twice, but do not comment whether it is true or false. (Alternatively, display the three statements on the whiteboard.)

The rest of the class decide which statement is correct (only one of each statements in the four sets is true).

Give the children a few minutes to discuss this with a partner, then ask for a show of hands for each statement in turn.

Discuss with the class which statement is the true statement, and why.

(m) *Tell us what you think 'improper' usually means. Do you see any link between that meaning and the meaning in 'improper fraction'?*

Does everyone agree with that explanation? Does anyone disagree?

Can you explain Harry's idea in your own words?

Now that you've talked about that statement together, are you confident that it is false?

Does talking together help you get clearer about what something means?

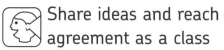
Support: Give examples, using smaller or less complex numbers.

Extend: Ask for further statements that might or might not be true and encourage the class to discuss them.

Plenary

Refer to the brainstorm list.

Write up some incomplete sentences in which the missing word is one of those on display. Children work in pairs to agree on what they think the missing word is, then write it on their wipe boards and hold them up to you.

(m) *"In the number 4.05 there are five …?" Agree with your partner what the missing word is.*

(☺) *Some people have written 'percentage', and some have put 'per cent'. Who can explain which is correct, and why?*

Assessment for learning

Can the children	If not
(m) Explain why $\frac{896}{12}$ is an improper fraction and $1\frac{1}{3}$ isn't?	(m) Provide some work that involves sorting numbers into improper fractions, proper fractions and mixed numbers. Encourage children to use the relevant vocabulary.
(☺) Repeat another child's explanation about one of the true or false statements?	(☺) Do some exercises with the class in which children repeat back to you (or each other) made-up sentences on any topic. Move on to simple explanations such as 'eight 8s must be 64, because it is double four 8s, which is 32'.
(☺) Speak loudly and clearly when putting forward a point of view?	(☺) Give the class practice in talking about something they are comfortable with – mountain bikes, music or their collection of seashells.

Fractions and equivalent percentages

Classroom technique: Talking partners

Learning objectives

(m) Maths
Relate fractions to their percentage representations

Speaking and listening
'Make decisions and talk about them'
Use the processes and language of decision making

Personal skills
'Think about what you have learned'
Improve learning and performance: reflect on learning

(w) Words and phrases
whole, part, fraction, simplify, equivalent, equal, the same, per cent, %, percentage

(r) Resources
display copy of RS8
for each pair:
fraction cards cut from RS7
copies of RS8
counters
copies of RS9
(optional)

Introduction

Use the 'Goldfish bowl' technique (p14) to demonstrate a game. Ask one group of four (made up of two pairs) to play, while the rest of the class stand or sit in a circle around them and watch.

Give the group a set of sixteen fraction cards (cut from RS7), the first percentages board copied from RS8 and counters in two different colours. Children shuffle the cards and place them face down on the table.

The pairs take turns to pick up a fraction card. They agree where to place it on the equivalent percentage value on the board (note that there are two of each value, so, initially, there are choices to be made). After laying down a card, they cover it with a counter in their colour to keep track of their own lines. The aim is to make lines of three or four in their own colour.

> **Talking partners**
> Remind children to discuss and agree together what to do: neither partner should allow the other to take overall control.

5 1%	10%	75%	20%
75%	2 %/4	5 1%	90%
30%	20%	30%	2 %/4
70%	190%	10%	70%

Play continues until all the cards are used up. Pairs work out their scores: lines of three score three points, and lines of four score four points. The highest total score wins.

(m) If $\frac{1}{10}$ is 10%, what is $\frac{2}{10}$?

(m) How can you change 75% to a fraction? How can you simplify that?

Groups of four

Organise the class into groups of four to play the game in pairs.

(m) How do you work out what percentage is equal to that fraction?

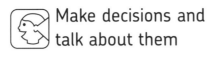

How do the two of you decide where to place your card? Are you sharing the decision making?

What are you learning about percentages and fractions?

Support: Provide children with the 'counting stick' on RS9 (marked with basic fraction and percentage equivalents) and help them use it.

Extend: Children replace some of the fraction cards with decimal equivalents and then play the game again.

Differentiation

Less confident children can simply use fractions where the denominator is 100: "95% is $\frac{95}{100}$." Challenge other children to use simplified fractions.

U&A Use reasoning and logic

Help children explain their reasoning as they work out these equivalents: "10% is $\frac{1}{10}$, so 5% is $\frac{1}{20}$."

Plenary

Finally, play a game against the class, using the second percentages board on RS8. Instead of using fraction cards, players simply say a fraction that is equivalent to the percentage they want to cover.

You say that 12% is $\frac{12}{100}$. How do you simplify that fraction?

Can $\frac{99}{100}$ be simplified? Why not?

Tell your partner which percentage I should cover next, and why.

Tell your partner whether you are more sure about converting percentages to fractions today than you were yesterday.

Assessment for learning

Can the children

Give fraction equivalents for 10%, 30% and 80%? For 25% and 75%?

Explain how to work out these equivalents?

Pinpoint one new fact they have learned in this session?

If not

Revise the idea that percentages are like fractions in that everything is seen in terms of hundredths. Use the 'counting stick' model (see RS9) to establish simple equivalents.

Use the 'Peer tutoring' technique (p8): ask confident children to explain how they work out an equivalence, then ask less confident children to try this method for themselves and describe it back to their 'tutors'.

Ask children to try to notice during their next lesson when a new fact or idea is 'entering their head'. Give them space at the end of the lesson to talk about this.

Identifying decimal numbers

Classroom technique: Rotating roles

Learning objectives

(m) Maths
Know what each digit represents in a decimal number

Speaking and listening
'Share ideas and reach agreement as a group'
Share and discuss ideas and reach consensus

Personal skills
'Work cooperatively with others'
Work with others: work cooperatively with others

(w) Words and phrases
digit, decimal point, decimal place, greater than, less than, ones, tenths, hundredths

(r) Resources
display copy of RS10
for each group:
set of cards cut from RS10

Choosing numbers
Zero counts as a digit, but remind children that, conventionally, we do not use a zero in the hundredths place: we write 3.4, not 3.40. Children may choose the same digit more than once.

Filling in the blanks
The blanks on RS10 are there for the children to fill in as they please. Help them think about how to use these open questions to extract useful information: "Is it between 3 and 5?"

Reaching consensus
Ask children to challenge each other if they disagree with what is said and encourage them to check with their peers to see if they agree with the statements made.

Rotating roles
Children will get turns asking questions and answering them.

Introduction

Children work in pairs. Each pair uses any three digits to make a number of the form $\square.\square\square$. Write up eight of their numbers.

4.52	3.08
1.56	2.31
7.08	1.99
2.07	0.62

Choose one of the eight numbers to be your 'mystery number' and write it down secretly. The class are going to ask questions to identify this number.

Display the first question on RS10 for the class to read out.

Answer this question yourself and help the class use the information to eliminate numbers. Cross out or cover eliminated numbers.

Continue like this with the other questions until the children have identified your number.

Finally, reveal your mystery number.

(m) *Which of these numbers are less than 5.3? How do you know that?*

(m) *In this number, what is the digit in the tenths place?*

(speaking) *Discuss with your neighbour whether those two numbers are both greater than 3.7.*

Groups of four

Pairs join together to work in groups of four. Each child in the group chooses two or three numbers, as before, and writes them on a shared sheet of paper, resulting in a total of eight to twelve numbers. Give each group a set of question cards cut from RS10 to spread out on the table, face up.

One child chooses a number in secret, and the rest of the group take turns to pick a question and ask it, aiming to eliminate items and identify the chosen number.

Children take turns to choose a number.

(m) *How do you work out whether a number is greater than 4.15?*

(≋) *If you two don't agree about that number, how could you convince each other?*

(☺) *Do you need help with filling the blank in that question?*

Support: Work with two digits such as 3.4.

Extend: Aim to find the chosen number with a maximum of only two or three questions. Work with four digits such as 3.402.

Plenary

Assessment
This helps you assess how well children understand decimal numbers, which is particularly useful if you have not managed to observe all groups during the session.

As a class, discuss which questions are useful in seeking to identify a mystery number and talk about strategies for filling in the blanks in the question cards.

Choose two questions from RS10 and ask children to write on their wipe boards a decimal number where the answer to both is 'Yes'.

(≋) *Is it ever a good idea to ask a question naming a specific number – for example, "Is it 4.02?" Tell your neighbour what you think.*

Assessment for learning

Can the children

(m) Say the value of each digit in 4.53, 6.05 and 4.09 and use this knowledge to order the numbers?

If not

(m) Use a base board as shown to display a decimal number, then rearrange the same digits to make a different number. Discuss the changes made and how they affect the value of each digit.

Ones	tenths	hundredths
4	5	7

(≋) Let another child finish what they are saying without interrupting?

(≋) Model the 'bad behaviour' by asking another adult to tell you something and interrupting them deliberately. Discuss how this may make the interrupted person feel.

(☺) Check with others in the group before eliminating a number?

(☺) Make sure you check with everybody when doing this as a class activity and allow space to children who disagree. Comment on what you are doing so that children can begin to identify it as desirable behaviour.

Finding fractions

Classroom technique: Heads or tails

Learning objectives

(m) Maths
Relate fractions
to division

(speaking) Speaking and listening
'Join in a discussion with
the whole class'
Contribute to whole-class
discussion

(personal) Personal skills
'Try different ways
to tackle a problem'
Organise work: use different
approaches to tackle a problem

(w) Words and phrases
fraction, decimal,
mixed number, divide, half,
quarter, eighth, third, sixth,
twelfth, tenth, hundredth,
method, check

(r) Resources
square tiles (optional)

Time to think
Allow children time to think
before taking responses.

Modelling
Illustrate some of the
explanations by dividing
up a grid of 12 squares.
$\frac{1}{2}$ of 12 is 6.
$\frac{1}{4}$ of 12 is 3.

Equivalent fractions
Children may derive fractions
that are equivalent – for example,
$\frac{4}{12}$ and $\frac{1}{3}$. Acknowledge these,
but don't, at this stage, expect
children to understand rules for
generating equivalent fractions
such as 'multiply top and bottom
by the same amount'.

Heads or tails
Warn children that you will be
using this technique in the
plenary so that pairs are equally
prepared to offer an explanation.

Introduction

Children work in pairs to find any fractions of 12 that
they can, noting how they work out each fraction.

Collect and record some of these fractions on the
board, together with explanations of how the children
worked them out.

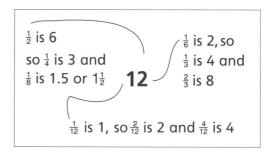

Give names to the methods and write these up on the
board: 'halving repeatedly', 'dividing by 10', and so on.

(m) *This pair says that an eighth of 12 is 1.5.
Can you say that as a mixed number?*

(m) *Halve 12 twice to get $\frac{1}{4}$ of 12.
Why does this work?*

(speaking) *Does everyone understand that explanation?
Does anyone have any questions about it?*

Pairs

Ask pairs to choose 24, 48 or 60 and work out
fractions of the chosen number. Suggest that they
try some of the methods written up on the board.

(m) *How does multiplication or division help you
find one third of 60?*

(personal) *What method have you used there?
What method will you try next?*

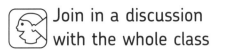
Support: Children choose their own numbers and find a half and a quarter of each one.

Extend: Give children calculators to explore 'harder' fractions with: "I used halving to find $\frac{1}{16}$ of 24. It is 1.5."

Heads or tails
Use this technique when asking pairs to explain their workings.

Illustrating the work
You could draw up a chart to show the links between fractions of 12, 24, 48 and 60.

	12	24	48	60
$\frac{1}{2}$	6	12	24	30
$\frac{1}{4}$	3	6	12	15

Plenary

Collect and record on the board some of the fractions the children have found.

Discuss connections between fractions of 12 and fractions of 24, 48 or 60. For example, $\frac{1}{2}$ of 12 is 6 and $\frac{1}{2}$ of 24 is 12 – twice as much.

Tell the class how you found one eighth of 48.

How can we check that answer?

Does anyone have a different way of doing it?

Assessment for learning

Can the children

Use repeated halving and dividing by 10 and 100 to find $\frac{1}{2}$, $\frac{1}{4}$, $\frac{1}{8}$, $\frac{1}{10}$ and $\frac{1}{100}$ of various whole numbers?

Volunteer a contribution to the class discussion?

Try a method they say they have not used before?

If not

Give children practice at dividing up rectangles drawn on squared paper and help them make links between division and fractions: "Divide 12 into 3 bits. $\frac{1}{3}$ of 12 is 4, and 12 ÷ 3 = 4." Work with a base board, moving digit cards from one position to an adjacent one and describing this in terms of 'tenths' and 'ten times'. Check the results with a calculator.

Make a mental note of children who do not volunteer contributions. Make sure you include them by asking them questions later they can answer confidently or by asking their partner to report what they have said (see 'Ticket to explain', p11).

Ask a child who is happy with a particular method to demonstrate it and to help their 'pupil' try it out on various numbers (see 'Peer tutoring', p8).

Self and peer assessment

Lesson 5: Using fraction number words	I think	My partner thinks
(m) I can recognise an improper fraction.		
I can explain why 0.53 is greater than 0.4.		
I can confidently say three facts about fractions and decimals.		

Lesson 6: Fractions and equivalent percentages	I think	My partner thinks
(m) I can say the fractions that are equivalent to: 10%, 70% and 25%		
I can explain how I work out the percentage equivalent of $\frac{3}{10}$.		
I can say one thing that I have learned today.		

Name _____

Lesson 7: Identifying decimal numbers	I think	My partner thinks
(m) I can say the value of each digit in 4.53, 6.05 and 4.09 and order the numbers.		
I let someone else finish what they are saying without interrupting.		
I check that others in my group agree with my decisions.		

Lesson 8: Finding fractions	I think	My partner thinks
(m) I can find $\frac{1}{4}$ and $\frac{1}{8}$ of 24.		
I am willing to say something in the class discussion.		
I have tried out a new method for finding fractions.		

Self and peer assessment

Word Bank
March
April
May
June
September
October
November
December

Addition and subtraction

Learning objectives

	Lessons			
	9	**10**	**11**	**12**
Ⓜ Maths objectives				
use an empty number line to add and subtract	●			
practise mental calculations		●		
add several small numbers mentally			●	
use appropriate number operations to solve problems				●
Ⓢ Speaking and listening skills				
share and discuss ideas and reach consensus	●			
use precise language to explain ideas or give information		●		
reach a common understanding with a partner			●	
contribute to small-group discussion				●
Ⓟ Personal skills				
work with others: overcome difficulties and recover from mistakes	●			
work with others: work cooperatively with others		●		
organise work: use different approaches to tackle a problem			●	
organise work: plan a sequence of work				●

About these lessons

Lesson 9: Mental calculation strategies

 Use an empty number line to add and subtract

There are many ways to do addition and subtraction calculations on an empty number line. In this activity, children discuss how to do such problems, supported by their partner and group.

 Share and discuss ideas and reach consensus

Classroom technique: Peer tutoring

Children work in mixed-ability pairs. If one child understands an aspect of the work that the other doesn't, they work together in a tutor/pupil relationship to make sure that they both share their understanding. The purpose behind the sharing and discussing of ideas – that of understanding a number line technique – gives focus to children's talk.

 Work with others: overcome difficulties and recover from mistakes

Children use the empty number line to do calculations and to check their answers. They then correct any mistakes themselves. Acknowledging to children that everyone makes mistakes and encouraging them to check and correct any errors gives them responsibility for their own learning, rather than leaving it in the hands of the teacher.

Lesson 10: Using two-digit numbers

 Practise mental calculations

Practice in mental calculations can be made more enjoyable by contriving a purpose for doing them. Games such as the one in this lesson give children a motive for thinking about which calculation will give them a 'good' result and then carrying out the calculation.

 Use precise language to explain ideas or give information

Classroom technique: One between two

Children take turns to choose and record numbers. The 'Chooser' instructs their partner what to write or record with the pencil and how to carry out any necessary calculations. If the 'Recorder' is not sure of what is wanted, they ask for further explanation. This structure requires children to communicate clearly and precisely.

 Work with others: work cooperatively with others

Maths games – even when they are competitive – encourage children to work cooperatively as they take turns, share resources and aim for the same outcome.

Lesson 11: Adding several small numbers

 Add several small numbers mentally

This is another game that offers a motive for thinking about, and then carrying out, calculations. Having a choice about which digits to add to reach a total means that children do several quick estimates/calculations to find a set of digits that 'work'.

 Reach a common understanding with a partner

Classroom technique: Heads or tails

This technique encourages pairs to work together and helps prevent one child relying too much on the other. Both must understand the decisions they have made and the reasons behind them, because neither partner knows who will be called on to give an explanation to the class.

Organise work: use different approaches to tackle a problem

The class share methods for adding several numbers, and children are asked to try one of the methods that was unfamiliar to them until then. This helps children acquire a repertoire of calculation strategies and develop a flexible attitude.

Lesson 12: Solving word problems

Use appropriate number operations to solve problems

This is a challenging exercise in extracting meaning from print, analysing what information is needed, then deciding which calculations to do to get that information.

 Contribute to small-group discussion

Classroom technique: Talking partners

In 'Talking partners', children work together informally, with no structured roles. This technique helps children develop and practise the skills of collaboration, where each contributes to discussion of the group task and to decision making.

 Organise work: plan a sequence of work

Children working together on a 'real-life' problem have to decide what information they need, how to extract it and in what order to do this – exactly the same procedure that they will encounter when dealing with mathematical tasks in the adult world.

Mental calculation strategies
Classroom technique: Peer tutoring

Learning objectives

m Maths
Use an empty number line to add and subtract

Speaking and listening
'Share ideas and reach agreement with your partner'
Share and discuss ideas and reach consensus

Personal skills
'Get over difficulties and mistakes'
Work with others: overcome difficulties and recover from mistakes

w Words and phrases
add, addition, total, double, subtract, subtraction, difference, minus, equals, answer, method, solution, check

r Resources
for each pair:
copy of RS11
0–9 dice

Introduction

Revise the use of an empty number line for doing addition and subtraction calculations. Present a calculation and invite children to discuss in pairs how they would do this on an empty number line. Emphasise that there is often more than one way to reach a solution.

Working mentally
If children prefer to work mentally, acknowledge this and ask them to use the empty number line to demonstrate their mental processes.

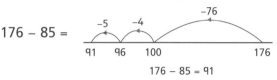

$176 - 85 =$

Method 1: Jumping back 85 from 176
$176 - 85 = 91$

Method 2: Finding the difference between 85 and 176
$176 - 85 = 15 + 76 = 91$

Read out the number sentence with your partner and talk about what it means. Approximately how big do you think the answer will be?

Pairs

Children work in mixed-ability pairs, with a copy of RS11 each. For each question, children roll the dice as many times as there are empty boxes and write the digits on the sheet. They then discuss together how to put the digits in the boxes to form a calculation that makes sense.

Using the dice numbers
For example,
dice numbers 4 7 1 9
Arranging them as follows
4 1 + 7 9
gives an easy calculation.

Pairs discuss how to do the calculation, mentally or using an empty number line, do it and write the answer in the oval on RS11.

Ask pairs to check their answer in one of two ways. If they found it mentally, they check by using an empty number line. If they used the line the first time, they use it again, but with a different method, to help them identify and correct any errors.

Peer tutoring
Observe children at work and identify those who are confident and accurate with the empty number line. Give these children the title of 'Number Line Expert' and ask them to work with individuals needing support. This may mean rearranging some pairs halfway through the lesson.

Pairs continue in the same way with the other questions.

m What numbers will you put on your number line? Tell me about the jumps you are going to do.

m With that calculation, what do you need to find out?

m Is there another way you could do that calculation? Would it be any easier?

Tell your partner how you would work out that answer.

How are you both working on that problem? Expert, are you going to show your pupil what to do or tell them so they do it themselves?

Support: Use peer tutors – either the partner or a child from another partnership – to model and teach empty number line methods.

Extend: Rather than rolling a dice, suggest that children choose the digits themselves, aiming to form calculations that will challenge them.

Plenary

Pairs get together in groups of four and talk about their experience of working in this way.

Children think in private about what they have learned from the experience.

Experts, do you think you have learned anything from being a tutor?

Those of you who were helped by a tutor, do you think you understand more now about using an empty number line?

Topics for discussion
- what it was like writing their own calculations
- what it was like being a Number Line Expert
- what it was like being tutored by a Number Line Expert
- how confident they feel about using the empty number line

Number Line Experts
The title of 'Expert' can be carried over into other lessons, though it is important not to overdo the amount of tutoring children do. Try to identify other children as other kinds of Expert, so that the sense of achievement it gives is shared as widely as possible.

Assessment for learning

Can the children

Use an empty number line to carry out or check a calculation?

Tell their partner how they would use an empty number line to do a calculation?

Accept the support of a peer tutor?

If not

Ask children to talk you through some calculations they can do mentally and model these on an empty number line while they watch. This helps children see how the number line models and supports mental strategies.

See if they can actually draw and use the number line. As they do so, put into words for them what they are doing.

Find out who they would like to help them and try using this person as a tutor. Consider using the child as an 'Expert' in some other area of learning (perhaps not mathematics) to help them warm to the idea.

Using two-digit numbers

Classroom technique: One between two

Partition into hundreds, tens and ones
Children are likely to use a range of strategies, but this one will be useful to fall back on when none of the others are suitable.

One between two
One child instructs their partner about which calculation to do, talking them through any necessary calculations on scrap paper.
For their next turn, children swap roles.

Game 1 and Game 2
RS12 has space to record two games. Some groups might manage two games in one session – or they can play a second game at a later date.

Introduction

Work with the class on some additions and subtractions involving two-digit numbers. Take the opportunity to revise various mental and jottings strategies.

(m) *You want to add 27 to 165. If you added 30 first, how much would you then have to take off?*

Talk your partner through subtracting 65 on an empty number line.

Groups of four

Children work in groups of four (two teams of two). Give each group a copy of RS12, a calculator and two coloured pens or pencils.

The game starts with a total of 50.

Team 1

Child A rolls two 0–9 dice and arranges the numbers to make a two-digit number (this can include numbers with 0 in the tens place, such as 04).

Child A instructs Child B either to add this to, or subtract it from, the running total. The aim is to end up with a number that is a multiple of 5 or 10.

Child B records the two-digit number and new total on RS12, in their team's colour.

Number made with dice	+ or –?	Total so far
		50
31	+	81
24	+	105

This scores as it is a multiple of 5.

Team 2

Team 2 checks Team 1's calculations with a calculator. If the new total is a multiple of 5 or 10, Team 1 scores a point.

Team 2 now has its turn. The children do the same as the children in Team 1, starting with the new total.

Play continues like this until both teams have had eight turns.

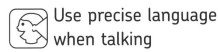
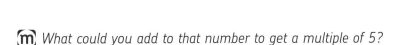 *What could you add to that number to get a multiple of 5?*

Explain to your partner why you arranged the dice numbers to make 13 rather than 31.

What can you do that will make the game enjoyable for everybody? And what would make the game a real pain for other people?

Support: Use one dice and multiply the result by 10. Add this to, or subtract it from, the running total. If the new total is a multiple of 50, the team scores a point.

Extend: Start the game with a total of 500. Aim for numbers ending in 4 or 7 or multiples of 3 and 8.

Plenary

Ticket to explain
You could use 'Ticket to explain' (p11) when discussing methods.

Present a calculation that might come up in the game. Pairs confer together about how they would do this calculation and suggest possible methods.

Why does that method work? Can you draw a diagram on the board to show us?

Assessment for learning

Can the children

Add 25, 39 or 67 to a two- or three-digit number? Subtract those numbers?

Talk their partner through adding 31, 45 or 78 to a two- or three-digit number?

Wait patiently when it is the other team's turn?

If not

Revise partitioning, using an empty number line to do such calculations.

Use an empty number line yourself to do a calculation and get children to talk to a partner about what you are doing, and how it models the problem.

Encourage children to find strategies to make waiting more interesting, such as doing the same calculation as the other team, mentally.

Adding several small numbers
Classroom technique: Heads or tails

Learning objectives

m **Maths**
Add several small numbers mentally

Speaking and listening
'Reach an understanding with your partner'
Reach a common understanding with a partner

Personal skills
'Try different ways to tackle a problem'
Organise work: use different approaches to tackle a problem

w **Words and phrases**
add, addition, plus, total, double, near double, add ... and adjust, calculate, explain, method, strategy, jotting

r **Resources**
two 0–20 dice

Tell your partner
Children turn to their neighbour and tell them their answer, and how they got there.

Heads or tails
Use 'Heads or tails' (p12) to ensure that both partners are equally involved and able to offer an explanation.
Asking for other methods that would work means the rest of the class must listen to the explanation.

All abilities
Involve pairs of all abilities in describing their methods. There are likely to be some calculations simple enough for even low-attaining children to feel confident about explaining, and it is important they have opportunities to speak to the class.
Methods of adding:
– doubling
– using near doubles like 9 and 8
– looking for pairs that make 10
– adding 9 is like adding 10 and subtracting 1

Introduction

Present the class with trios of digits such as 4, 6, 8 for children to add together mentally.

m *Why is it helpful if you know the number bonds to 10 really well? How can you use them to add those numbers?*

Whole class/Pairs

This game is for the whole class, with the children working in pairs. Each child chooses three single-digit numbers to write down so that each pair has six numbers altogether. (The numbers can be repeated.)

Roll two 0–20 dice and add the numbers with the class. Write up the total. Pairs try to make that total by adding all or any of their six digits.

Pairs who succeed score a point.

Play several rounds and, occasionally, ask one or more pairs to explain to the class their method of adding their digits. Ask for alternative methods that would also work.

Different methods Aim for 24	
6 2 7	**9 4 5**
Method 1	Method 2
$4 + 5 + 9 + 6 = 24$	$4 + 6 + 9 + 5 = 24$
(Add 4 and 5 ➤ 9, then use doubling to add on 9 ➤ 18 add 6 ➤ 24)	(Use pairs that make 10 4 and 6 ➤ 10 add 9 ➤ 19 add 5 ➤ 24)

Write up general descriptions for these methods so that you and the children can refer back to them.

m *Are some digits more useful than others? Why/Why not?*

Tell us why you started with the 9. Which of you suggested it?

Explain why you think it is a bad idea to have lots of the same digit.

Which of these methods do you use most often? Which method don't you ever use?

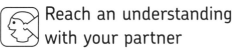
Support: Provide a number line for children to use to keep track of their calculations.

Extend: Each child writes down three numbers below 20 (rather than single-digit numbers) to use in their additions.

Plenary

Present six digits and roll both dice, as before, to establish a total. Discuss different ways to use some of these digits to reach the total.

Each pair tries out one of the methods discussed that they would not normally use.

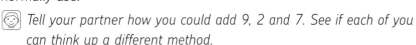 *Tell your partner how you could add 9, 2 and 7. See if each of you can think up a different method.*

Trying out new methods
Offering children challenges such as this encourages them to reflect on what they know and do as well as on what they don't know and don't do.

Assessment for learning

Can the children	**If not**
Add several digits accurately and quickly?	Suggest that children look for a pair or pairs that they can add, then use jottings or an empty number line to add on the rest.
Explain clearly how they did their calculations?	Offer an explanation yourself and ask pairs to repeat it.
Identify and try a method they do not generally use?	Work with the class on describing and naming mental methods and get the children to vote for their favourite and least favourite methods. Then try out the least favourite to perform a particular calculation.

Solving word problems

Classroom technique: Talking partners

Learning objectives

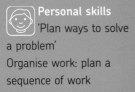

Maths
Use appropriate number operations to solve problems

Speaking and listening
'Join in a discussion with a small group'
Contribute to small-group discussion

Personal skills
'Plan ways to solve a problem'
Organise work: plan a sequence of work

Words and phrases
calculate, calculation, method, strategy, jotting, answer, operation, check

Resources
for each group:
display copy of RS13
copies of RS13 (optional)
calculators (optional)

Task

Scribe the elements of the task for the children so that they can reflect on them:
– the number of coaches needed
– how many adults will go with the children
– the total cost of the outing

Talking partners

Put together groups of three children who have previously worked together in given roles and have the confidence to tackle this new, less structured task.

What information?

Children may need help working out what information they need to find, and in what order. If necessary, prompt them to work out the number of people on the outing before thinking about the number of coaches needed.

Multi-step problems

Children will need to use several operations to answer all the questions – not all of them addition. It is important that children have experience of identifying the operation they need to do, rather than always being told.

Introduction

Display a copy of RS13 and read it through with the children.

Discuss the imaginary scenario and establish with the children what their task is.

Why do we need to know the number of coaches?

What else do we need to know? Talk about this with your partner.

Groups of three

Children work on the task in groups of three, sharing the work fairly between them.

Children may use calculators, but remind them to assess whether they could do the calculations as easily without them.

What calculation do you need to do for that?

You are adding. Could you multiply?

Do you all understand why Joss is adding up four lots of £250? Ask him to explain.

What would be helpful to do first? And then?

What question are you now ready to answer? And what question can you answer next?

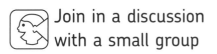
Support

This work is quite complex, and children who are not used to such an independent working style may need support in talking it through. Encourage them to draw diagrams to help solve the problems.

Support: Talk through how to find out the number of children on the outing, the number of adults needed and how many coaches would be needed.

Extend: Children work out the cost per child of a half-day or full-day outing and argue a case for choosing one or the other option. They draw up a timetable for the outing.

Plenary

One or more groups present their answers, their 'proposal' and their methods of calculation and explain how they shared out the work.

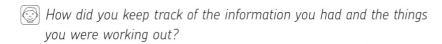 *Explain how you worked out that you need 19 adults on the trip.*

How did you keep track of the information you had and the things you were working out?

Assessment for learning

Can the children

 See which operation(s) they need to do in order to establish a piece of information?

Ask another group member for an explanation when they don't understand something?

Clearly identify the first thing to do towards the 'proposal'?

If not

Ask children to tell you what numbers they are dealing with and what they represent (children, coaches, and so on). Help them gain a clear picture of the situation and 'feel' whether it is about adding or dividing.

Remind children that they are sharing the work and that this includes sharing the understanding of what they know and need to know.

Suggest that they write down the three facts they need to put together their 'proposal'. Discuss with them what they need to find out to establish the first fact.

Self and peer assessment

Lesson 9: Mental calculation strategies	I think	My partner thinks
(m) I can use an empty number line to do this calculation:		
I can tell my partner how I would use an empty number line to do that calculation.		
I try hard to explain clearly when I work as an Expert.		

Lesson 10: Using two-digit numbers	I think	My partner thinks
(m) I can add [ ] to [ ].		
I can tell my partner how to add [ ] to [ ].		
I let the other team take as long as they need when it is their turn.		

Name _____

Lesson 11: Adding several small numbers	I think	My partner thinks
(m) I can add digits accurately.		
(☺) I can explain what I do in my head when I add small numbers.		
(☺) I am prepared to try a method I do not often use.		

Lesson 12: Solving word problems	I think	My partner thinks
(m) I can choose which operation to do to find out a fact I need.		
(☺) I discuss a problem with my group before starting to work on it.		
(☺) I can work out the first thing to do when I am working on a problem.		

Self and peer assessment

Listening Chart

Word Bank.

March | April | May | June

September | October | November | December

Multiplication and division

Learning objectives

	Lessons			
	13	**14**	**15**	**16**
ⓜ Maths objectives				
understand the operation of multiplication and its relationship to addition	●	●		
find factors for any number to 100			●	
solve simple word problems involving numbers and quantities				●
Speaking and listening skills				
explain and justify thinking	●		●	
share and discuss ideas and reach consensus		●		
contribute to small-group discussion				●
Personal skills				
improve learning and performance: reflect on learning	●			
work with others: work cooperatively with others		●		
work with others: discuss and agree ways of working			●	
improve learning and performance: develop confidence in own judgements				●

About these lessons

Lesson 13: Addition and multiplication links

(m) Understand the operation of multiplication and its relationship to addition

An ideas map can help reveal what children know well, what they partially know and what they have not yet met or understood. This lesson suggests how to use an ideas map to explore ideas about multiplication.

Explain and justify thinking

Classroom technique: Talking partners

Children who have previously worked in given roles now work on a collaborative activity without these defined roles. Sharing a task, they need to explain their ideas to each other and agree together how to proceed with their work.

Improve learning and performance: reflect on learning

Brainstorming ideas about multiplication and discussing how to link them together helps children reflect on what they understand about this area of mathematics. As they hear other children talk, they may come to see aspects of the topic that they realise they don't yet grasp fully.

Lesson 14: Multiplying numbers

(m) Understand the operation of multiplication and its relationship to addition

In this lesson, children investigate sums of three consecutive numbers. Looking for a quick way to calculate these leads them to use multiplication.

Share and discuss ideas and reach consensus

Classroom technique: Think, pair, share

This technique gives children time to think on their own, rehearse their thoughts with a partner and then discuss these in a larger group. Working together in this larger group, the children need to reach agreement about the task in hand.

Work with others: work cooperatively with others

Children work in pairs, then in groups of four, to share their ideas for solving a problem. The structure and the shared aim help them practise working cooperatively.

Lesson 15: Exploring factors

(m) Find factors for any number to 100

Children need to develop the idea that some numbers such as 48 are rich in factors. Thinking about the best numbers to choose for their Bingo board helps children develop this feel for numbers and their factors.

Explain and justify thinking

Classroom technique: Heads or tails

Pairs are invited to the front of the class to explain their ideas or solutions. When they get to the front, the toss of a coin decides which of them will do the talking. This means that both children must be prepared to talk to the class and offer an explanation of their ideas.

Work with others: discuss and agree ways of working

Pairs of children discuss and agree how to share the task of investigating which numbers will be 'useful' in their Bingo game and then agree on a set of numbers for their new improved board.

Lesson 16: Division word problems

(m) Solve simple word problems involving numbers and quantities

In this lesson, children think about the information in division word problems and focus on formulating appropriate answers.

Contribute to small-group discussion

Classroom technique: Devil's advocate

Statements – false or ambiguous as well as true – can be better than questions at provoking discussion. In this lesson, groups are presented with statements to agree or disagree with and to argue about.

Improve learning and performance: develop confidence in own judgements

In this lesson, the problems are already provided with solutions. The children's focus is on discussing which solution makes sense. Talking about the 'real-life' context can give children a better sense of what the problem is about and allow them to speak with confidence about their reasons for deciding on a solution.

Addition and multiplication links

Classroom technique: Talking partners

Learning objectives

(m) Maths
Understand the operation of multiplication and its relationship to addition

Speaking and listening
'Explain what you think and why you think it'
Explain and justify thinking

Personal skills
'Think about what you have learned'
Improve learning and performance: reflect on learning

(W) Words and phrases
multiple, multiplication, repeated addition, division, connect, connection, picture, graph, diagram, method, explain

(r) Resources
copy of RS14
whiteboard or flip chart
for each pair:
large sheets of sugar paper
sticky notes
material from previous years, such as workbooks (optional)

Making lists
This could be words that can mean the same thing ('times', 'multiply'); methods that can be used (doubling, grid method); pictures or images (jumps on a number line); or types of problem. Children might want to look at other material from previous years, such as workbooks or photographs of displays.

What's on the board
Tell children to use ideas from the board only if they are confident about what they mean.

Talking partners
Put children together who previously have worked in given roles (for instance, using 'One between two', p8).

Introduction

Have a time-limited class brainstorm of ideas connected with multiplication. Write up these ideas on the board.

Children talk to a neighbour about what these words mean. The neighbour either agrees or adds their own interpretation. They may also pick a word and acknowledge that they don't understand it.

(m) *You say that multiples are something to do with multiplication. Can you say what?*

Tell us why 'addition' is a good word to have on our list.

Pairs

Each child makes a list of what they know about multiplication, using items from the list on the board as appropriate and also adding their own.

Organise children in pairs to compare lists and add any new words, phrases or images they can think of. They record some of their ideas on large sticky notes.

(m) *I wonder if you could use a number line to show what repeated addition is.*

What do you mean by that word/picture?

Support: Provide children with RS14. They identify words with which they feel comfortable and copy them onto sticky notes. The connections that children see give you useful information about their level of understanding.

Extend: Ask for ideas about the relationship between multiplication and division.

U&A Recognising and
describing relationships
This is an important aspect of
mathematical thinking – and it
is worth telling the children so.

Ideas map
Keep the class map as a
reference. Add to it later in
the year or let it stand to
show the class how much
progress they have made
in their understanding of
multiplication. For more on
'Ideas maps' – see p12.

Plenary

Children read out one of their notes and add it to a class map about multiplication, using either a whiteboard or a large sheet of paper.

The class suggest connections between words or phrases on the map. Scribe these, with a line joining the words.

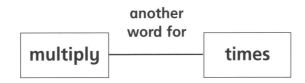

(m) *The link between 'multiplication' and 'division' says 'they are opposites'. Do you agree with that? What does it mean exactly?*

Tell me a way in which these ideas are connected.

How have you used what you learned about multiplication last year?

Assessment for learning

Can the children

(m) Think up a range of images, phrases or words connected with multiplication?

Explain connections between two different images, phrases or words?

Acknowledge when they don't understand something?

If not

(m) Note what is absent and plan teaching to focus on the vocabulary and ideas.

Provide these explanations yourself and ask children to repeat to their partners what you have said.

Work to develop the idea that it is fine not to know – perhaps by talking sometimes about what you yourself don't understand.

Multiplying numbers
Classroom technique: Think, pair, share

Learning objectives

Maths
Understand the operation of multiplication and its relationship to addition

Speaking and listening
'Share ideas and reach agreement as a group'
Share and discuss ideas and reach consensus

Personal skills
'Work cooperatively with others'
Work with others: work cooperatively with others

Words and phrases
add, sum, multiply, hypothesis, pattern, problem, solve, guess, formula, consecutive, relationship

Resources
for each group:
number fans
linking cubes
calculators (optional)

Paired work
Children work together to add the three numbers and show their answer with number fans.

Think, pair, share
Keep the timing sharp: three minutes for individuals, five minutes for pairs and ten minutes for groups of four.

Introduction

Ask the class for some trios of numbers and write them up. Include trios of consecutive numbers and establish which sets are, and which are not, consecutive. Check that everyone understands what you mean by 'consecutive'.

Present the challenge: "Find a quick way to add three consecutive numbers." Work with the class to add at least one such trio.

(m) *What are you doing first to add the numbers? Why is that?*

(m) *Does anyone start with the middle number?*

Groups of four

Ask individual children to choose any three consecutive numbers to add, then share their results with a partner.

Pairs then work together in groups of four to add further trios, looking for any patterns in their ways of working and their results.

(m) *How could you use multiplication rather than addition?*

(s) *What have you learned from this other pair?*

Support: Children work with numbers less than 10 or 20.

Extend: Children use calculators to check that their rule works with numbers of any size – for example, 999 + 1000 + 1001.

Investigate adding four consecutive numbers. Find out which of these numbers are the sums of three or four consecutive numbers: 6, 12, 30, 60.

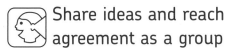
Plenary

Ask pairs for ideas about how to answer the challenge and anything else they have noticed. Record their ideas on the board.

If none of the children come up with the explanation that the sum of three consecutive numbers is the same as the middle number multiplied by 3, present it yourself.

Each child then chooses three new consecutive numbers and applies the rule 'multiply the middle number by 3'. They describe to their partner what happened.

(m) *I wonder if your method would work with any numbers. What about really big numbers?*

(☺) *This pair says: "Take the first number, add the same number on twice, then add 3." Explain how you would use their method to add 5, 6 and 7.*

(☺) *This group had a disagreement, but sorted it out. Please can you tell us how you did that?*

(☺) *Does everyone feel that they listened well to other people?*

Modelling with linking cubes

Make three sticks that show consecutive numbers and use them to show that the sum of three consecutive numbers is the middle number multiplied by 3. Move the 'extra' cube from the largest number to fill the gap in the smallest number. Both sticks become the same length as the middle one.

U&A Generalising

It is relatively easy for children to see that 8 + 9 + 10 = 3 x 9. It is much more difficult for them to see that this works for any number. It is unlikely that you will resolve this in one lesson. What is important is that the children discuss the connection between repeated addition and multiplication.

Assessment for learning

Can the children

(m) Use multiplication to find the sum of 19, 20 and 21? Or 149, 150 and 151?

(☺) Join in a discussion with their group of four?

(☺) Make good eye contact when talking or listening?

If not

(m) Try modelling the situation with linking cubes (as outlined above) or give children calculators to check their answers.

(☺) Give the group a 'talking stick' and ensure that each child has a turn with the stick, has their say and is listened to.

(☺) Consider whether there are psychological or cultural reasons why the child avoids eye contact. If not, make time for face-to-face discussions in pairs on other occasions.

Exploring factors

Classroom technique: Heads or tails

Learning objectives

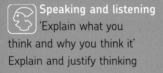 **Maths**
Find factors for any number to 100

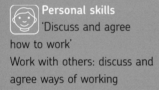 **Speaking and listening**
'Explain what you think and why you think it'
Explain and justify thinking

Personal skills
'Discuss and agree how to work'
Work with others: discuss and agree ways of working

Words and phrases
multiple, factor, prime, multiply, multiplication grid, product, systematic, find them all, record

Resources
for each pair:
copy of RS15
calculators
1–10 dice (or use a 0–9 dice and read 0 as 10)

Multiples

If the dice shows 1, roll again. Establish that any number can be seen as a multiple of itself – so a pair with 8 on their grid can cover it if you roll an 8.

Prime numbers

If children suggest numbers that are prime, take the opportunity to remind them what prime numbers are. Point out that prime numbers' only factors are themselves and 1, thus limiting their use in this game.

Heads or tails

Tell children early on in the lesson you will be using 'Heads or tails' (p12) in the plenary so that they know to prepare for either partner to speak.

Exploring numbers

Help children use a range of strategies for finding the dice numbers that work for a chosen Bingo number: dividing mentally, using knowledge of divisibility tests, dividing on a calculator, and so on.

Introduction

Children work in pairs. Each pair makes a 2 × 3 number grid, using one- or two-digit numbers, in preparation for a class game of 'Multiples Bingo'.

24	48	9
10	40	21

Roll a 1–10 dice and call out the number. Pairs who have a multiple of the dice number on their grid cross it out (only one number each time). The first pair to cross out all their numbers calls out: "Bingo!"

Give pairs time to reflect on the numbers on their board and how 'useful' they were and to change these numbers if they wish. Then play again.

(m) *What other numbers could you cross out with that dice number?*

Tell your partner a grid number that you could never cross out. Why couldn't you?

Pairs

Pairs of children investigate which Bingo numbers would be good to have on their boards. Give each pair a copy of RS15 to record all the numbers they investigate. After ten minutes, pairs make a new, larger, 2 × 4 Bingo board.

Suppose I wanted to use 37 because it is my favourite number. Would that help me win the game? Why not?

Think about a way of sharing the work fairly with your partner.

Support: Help children locate numbers on the multiplication grid (RS15) that appear more than twice and say what they are multiples of. Ask an available adult to work with children to prepare any explanations they might be asked to give in the plenary.

Explain what you think and why you think it

Extend: Ask the following question: "If the game were played with a 1–12, 1–20 or 1–50 spinner, what numbers would then be useful?" This will take children closer to a thorough search for factors.

Speaking skills

Encourage children to challenge each other and to defend their decisions.

Working systematically

Use your demonstration of systematic recording as a discussion point. Why and when is it important to be systematic?

	Bingo number	1-10 dice
😊	24	1 2 3 4 6 8
😐	16	1 2 4 8
☹	17 3	1 1 3

Plenary

Play a final game to test out the new boards.

Pairs come to the front and report on the numbers they investigated (using 'Heads or tails'). Record which numbers are 'great', 'OK' or 'useless' in terms of this game.

(m) *How can we be sure we have found all the dice numbers that will let us cross out that number?*

You disagree that 15 is a useful number. Where do you think it belongs then? Does anyone want to argue that 15 is useful?

Which is the most useful number we have found so far? Can you explain why 36 is a more useful number than 26?

Assessment for learning

Can the children

(m) Identify some or all of the factors of 12, 24, 36, 56?

Explain why they think 48 is a 'good' bingo number? Why 13 is a 'poor' number?

Show you how they are sharing the work with their partner?

If not

(m) Do further work on finding factors, perhaps dividing numbers by potential factors on a calculator and predicting the answer before pressing the '=' key.

Work on developing children's confidence by talking to an adult, a child partner or a small group initially if they lack confidence speaking to the class.

Do more work using 'One between two' (p8) to get children into the habit of sharing work equally with a partner. Ask effective pairs to model behaviour for the class.

Division word problems

Classroom technique: Devil's advocate

Learning objectives

(m) Maths
Solve simple word problems involving numbers and quantities

Speaking and listening
'Join in a discussion with a small group'
Contribute to small-group discussion

Personal skills
'Develop confidence about what you think and decide'
Improve learning and performance: develop confidence in own judgements

(w) Words and phrases
divide, division, answer, round up/down, correct, remainder, decimal, fraction, reason, explain

(r) Resources
for each group:
copies of RS16
calculator

Paired work
Children spend half a minute to think about this, then another half-minute discussing it with a partner.

Rounding
In this case, the calculation is 27 ÷ 6, and the answer is 4 teams, with 3 children left over.

Is rounding needed?
Children need to think about the kind of number required in the answer: are fractions or decimals more appropriate? Does the answer need rounding up or down? Is there a remainder to ignore or take account of? Two of the problems involve rounding, and two involve decimals or fractions.

Introduction

Write up the calculation: '27 ÷ 6 ='

Give children time to think about how they would solve this, then take suggestions about methods and answers. Establish three ways of showing the answer.

$$27 \div 6 = 4 \text{ r } 3 \text{ (remainder)}$$
$$27 \div 6 = 4.5 \text{ (decimal)}$$
$$27 \div 6 = 4\tfrac{3}{6} \text{ or } 4\tfrac{1}{2} \text{ (fraction)}$$

Introduce a word problem involving the same calculation: "27 children are asked to make teams of 6. How many teams can they make?" Talk about how doing the calculation is not enough to find the answer – you need to interpret it, and may need to round it up or down.

(m) *When you use a calculator to do that division, how does it 'show the remainder'?*

(S) *Talk to your partner about how you could turn the remainder into a fraction.*

Groups of three

Children work in groups of three. Give each child a copy of RS16, read out the problems and establish that for each of them the calculation is '129 ÷ 6', but that the results differ.

Model how to deal with the task in front of the class. Two children join you and read out the statements from Problem 1. As a group, agree which one is correct, and why, and discuss why the others are incorrect. Make sure you also model how to make a statement, saying why some answers are invalid.

Children tackle the remaining problems in their groups. One child reads out the different answers for Problem 2. They all discuss these, agree which is the correct answer and circle it. They then work together to make and record a statement, saying why the incorrect answers are not valid.

The other children take their turn as 'Reader', and the group share the solving of the remaining problems.

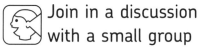

(m) *What has happened to the remainder in this problem? What does the remainder mean?*

(discussion) *How did you decide what the sensible answer was?*

(discussion) *If I asked any one of you why you chose that answer, could you all give me a reason?*

Support: Work with this group.

Extend: Children make up a further word problem to fit the calculation and decide on its answer and some possible invalid answers.

Plenary

Collect in some of the arguments against the invalid statements and discuss these.

Devil's advocate
Challenge children to clarify and express their reasoning by arguing for the incorrect answer.

(discussion) *Could the answer be 21 tents? Like with the eggs, you'll only manage to fill 21 tents with people.*

(face) *Why are you sure that this is the correct answer? Convince me.*

Assessment for learning

Can the children

(m) Identify the correct answers to the problems on RS16?

(discussion) Explain why the answer to Problem 2 must be rounded up?

(face) Stick by a sensible answer even when presented with a counter-argument?

If not

(m) Focus on interpreting and dealing with the word problem for a while.

(discussion) Use 'Peer tutoring' (p8): ask a child who does understand to explain it to those who do not.

(face) Try increasing the amount of debate and discussion about mathematical matters so that children get used to presenting ideas and sticking with them, or changing them, according to the arguments used.

Name _____

Self and peer assessment

Lesson 13: Addition and multiplication links	I think	My partner thinks
(m) I can draw pictures or diagrams to show ideas about multiplication.		
When working with an ideas map, I explain the connections between two different pictures or ideas.		
I am prepared to say when I don't understand something.		

Lesson 14: Multiplying numbers	I think	My partner thinks
(m) I can use multiplication to find the sum of 19, 20 and 21 and the sum of 149, 150 and 151.		
I talk in a group about my ideas.		
I look at somebody when they are talking to me.		

Name _____

Lesson 15: Exploring factors	I think	My partner thinks
(m) I can find some factors of 12, 24, 36 and 56.		
(👤) When I play 'Multiples Bingo', I can explain why I think a number is a 'good' Bingo number or a 'bad' Bingo number.		
(☺) I share work fairly when I work with a partner.		

Lesson 16: Division word problems	I think	My partner thinks
(m) I can tell when an answer to a division problem doesn't make sense.		
(👤) I can explain why an answer must be rounded up.		
(☺) I stick by an answer I'm sure about, even when somebody tries to convince me I'm wrong.		

Self and peer assessment

Listening Chart

Word Bank.

March   April   May   June

September   October   November   December

Handling data

Learning objectives

	Lessons			
	17	**18**	**19**	**20**
ⓜ Maths objectives				
discuss the probability of events	●			
develop understanding of the mode (most common item) of a set of data		●		
discuss a bar line chart showing the frequency of an event			●	
construct a bar line chart				●
Speaking and listening skills				
share and discuss ideas and reach consensus	●			
explain and justify thinking		●		
reach a common understanding with a partner			●	
contribute to whole-class discussion				●
Personal skills				
work with others: overcome difficulties and recover from mistakes	●			
improve learning and performance: reflect on learning		●		
improve learning and performance: take pride in work			●	
organise work: organise findings				●

About these lessons

Lesson 17: Exploring probabilities

 Discuss the probability of events

This activity helps children move from the stage of 'just guessing' to using evidence to judge the probability of an event occurring.

 Share and discuss ideas and reach consensus

Classroom technique: Talking partners

This technique helps children develop and practise the skills of collaboration in unstructured situations: sharing ideas and aiming to reach a mutually agreed conclusion.

 Work with others: overcome difficulties and recover from mistakes

Working with probability, where outcomes are often uncertain, is a different experience from number work where answers are correct or incorrect. In this lesson, children are encouraged to ask their peers for support and explanations if they are uncertain about any aspect of their work.

Lesson 18: Interpreting data

 Develop understanding of the mode (most common item) of a set of data

The best way for children to understand about making and reading graphs is through experience of actually collecting and recording data and, of course, discussing the results. In this lesson, children do just that.

 Explain and justify thinking

Classroom technique: Tell your partner

This technique encourages pairs to collaborate when working together on a task. Children talk with a partner, explaining and justifying their ideas about the way the graphs will develop. Then, when the graphs are complete, the children explore why they are the shape they are.

 Improve learning and performance: reflect on learning

Making and testing predictions about the frequency of events encourages children to focus on what they know or think they know. In discussing the results, children can be encouraged to articulate what they have gained from the lesson.

Lesson 19: Constructing charts

 Discuss a bar line chart showing the frequency of an event

Bar line charts serve much the same purpose as bar charts. Children need to be familiar with both types and practise interrogating them to extract information. This lesson provides opportunities to do this.

 Reach a common understanding with a partner

Classroom technique: Telephone conversation

Children sit back to back or with a barrier between them and give instructions about a bar line chart to enable their partner to draw one the same. As the listener cannot see the person speaking, children must listen to what is said and ask questions in order to understand each other.

 Improving learning and performance: take pride in work

Any piece of work can give children opportunities to feel proud about the way they have tackled it. Here, children are encouraged to take pride in being good communicators.

Lesson 20: Making charts independently

 Construct a bar line chart

When children make their own graph or chart from scratch, they understand at a deep level about the functions of its different parts. In this lesson, children work as individuals to make their own chart, supported by other children in the group who are using the same data to carry out the same task.

 Contribute to whole-class discussion

Classroom technique: Think, pair, share

Children consider a problem individually. They then explain their ideas to a partner. After the pairs have discussed the issue, they join another pair, share views and emerge with a group conclusion. This way, all children get an opportunity to express their views – and no one stays silent.

 Organise work: organise findings

Individual children collect and record simple data and share their ideas about how to present the group's combined data on a graph. They then work independently to make this graph. Both data collections and graphs are important ways of organising and presenting findings so that they are comprehensible to others.

Exploring probabilities

Classroom technique: Talking partners

Predicting

Encourage predictions in terms of 'good chance', 'poor chance', 'no chance' and 'even chance'. Ask children what reasons they have for their predictions. This can help other children develop their own understanding of probability.

Just a minute

Give pairs a minute (or less) to tell each other their prediction and their reason, agree a shared prediction and write this on a wipe board to hold up.

Talking partners

Put together pairs who have previously worked together and who have the confidence in each other to tackle the task.

Introduction

Display RS17 to the class. Turn a shuffled set of digit cards face up, one at a time.

Turn over one card, read the number and circle this number on RS17.

Ask the children to predict whether the next card you turn over will be a higher number or a lower number than the present one.

Assess what the majority of the class predict and mark this place on the scale.

Then turn over the next card and compare the actual result with the predicted one.

Repeat this process until all the cards are used up.

m *The first number is 8. Is it possible that the next number will be higher? How likely is it?*

What numbers are there left in my hand? Talk with your partner about whether there is a good chance that the next number will be higher than this one. How good a chance?

You can't always get the correct answer. Listen to what Kirsty says about the number cards and see if that helps you make better predictions.

Pairs

Give each pair of children two copies of RS18. Pairs agree the likelihood of the events listed for each partner in turn and record this by writing the letter above the scale. (The last three events can be filled in by the children themselves.)

Tell your partner one event you know is certain. How do you know that?

If you are finding this difficult, who could you talk to about it? Which pair can explain clearly how they are doing the work?

Support: Discuss ideas for the last three sentences.

Extend: Children add their own statements.

Plenary

Pairs read out a statement and say where on the scale they placed it, for each of them. Ask for reasons.

Pairs 'tell their partner' one thing they have learned in this lesson (this could be about maths, or working together, or about themselves).

Tell the class one statement you think is absolutely certain. Why do you think that?

Tell your partner what, if anything, was difficult about this lesson. What do you expect to find easier next time?

Tell your partner

Pairs take turns to talk for one minute about what they have got from the lesson. You can offer them a range of topics such as 'learning to judge probabilities', 'presenting my work' or 'working with a partner'.

Assessment for learning

Can the children

m Place the probability of an event on the scale and give reasons for placing it there?

Listen to and repeat what another child says?

Keep working even though some answers are uncertain – and they are more used to answers being 'correct' or 'incorrect'?

If not

m Ask children to think first about the events they know are certain or have 'no chance', then divide the others into 'good chance' or 'poor chance'.

Encourage pairs to practise this skill, using more familiar content such as 'what I did at the weekend' or 'my favourite team'.

Talk about the discomfort that uncertainty can cause and emphasise that having a go is important even when you don't know for certain that you are right.

Interpreting data

Classroom technique: Tell your partner

Why no '1'?
The chart shows dice totals of 2 to 12, because a score of 1 is impossible.

Tell your partner
Give children a minute to think about this in silence, then another minute to discuss it with their partner.

Rolling dice
Give children pot lids to roll their dice onto and say that if a dice falls off, they must roll again. This encourages carefulness. Alternatively, keep the dice in a transparent pot with a lid and turn it upside down.

Introduction

Display RS19 to the class. Roll two 1–6 dice a few times and record the totals on the chart.

Pairs tell their partner their prediction about the shape of the similar chart they are about to fill in and explain why they think that.

(m) *As I continue this graph, which total(s) will appear most often? Why?*

(m) *Explain to us why a total of 12 is less likely than a total of 6.*

Pairs

Give each pair of children a copy of RS19. Child A rolls two 1–6 dice, and Child B marks the total on the graph.

After ten rolls, the pair swaps roles and continues until both have had at least 30 rolls.

Then give children time to discuss with their partner how their graph's shape compares to the predicted shape.

(m) *What shape would the graph make if you rolled the dice 50 more times? Why would it be that shape?*

(s) *Tell Ama why you think your graph won't be straight across the top.*

Support: Remind children about 'counting on from the bigger number' if they are unsure of the number bonds to 12.

Extend: Children explain the shape of their graph.

Learning objectives

(m) **Maths**
Develop understanding of the mode (most common item) of a set of data

(s) **Speaking and listening**
'Explain what you think and why you think it'
Explain and justify thinking

(😊) **Personal skills**
'Think about what you have learned'
Improve learning and performance: reflect on learning

(W) **Words and phrases**
data, bar chart, label, title, axis, frequency, mode, range, probability, predict, mode

(r) **Resources**
display copy of RS19
display copy of RS20
for each pair:
copy of RS19
two 1–6 dice
pot lids

Plenary

Display RS20 to the class. Explain that you are going to combine all the children's results onto one graph.

Collect in data from all the pairs, for each dice total in turn (perhaps using a calculator), and record this on the graph.

As the graph develops, discuss its shape. Children make a prediction and tell their partner about the future shape of this graph.

Complete and discuss the graph and the children's predictions, using and explaining the word 'mode'.

(m) *How do you think this graph will compare to the ones you did? And why do you think that?*

(🐵) *Why is the shape of the graph roughly symmetrical?*

(🐵) *If we added three dice numbers instead of two, would the mode be more or less than 7?*

(☺) *If your neighbour's prediction was correct, congratulate them.*

(☺) *What do you think now about the predictions you made? How accurate were they?*

(☺) *Do you think if we were to do this activity again, you could make more accurate predictions?*

Spreadsheet

An alternative to filling in the communal graph is to enter the groups' data on a spreadsheet, set up to project its image for the class to see. This will draw the graph for you as well as totalling the scores.

Why this shape?

The graph will be approximately bell shaped, with few results for 2 and 12 and more for the numbers that can be achieved in several ways.

A valuable extension is to explore all the ways of making totals 2 to 12 with two dice – which produces a similarly shaped graph and accounts for the shape of the graphs from the children's experiments.

Assessment for learning

Can the children

(m) Predict whether the shape of the communal graph will be similar to their own graph?

(🐵) Explain why 2 or 12 are unlikely to be the mode?

(☺) Name one thing the lesson has taught them?

If not

(m) Ask an 'Expert' (see 'Peer tutoring', p8) to explain their ideas to the class.

(🐵) Talk about how many ways you can get 2 or 12 with two dice – then how many ways you can get 6, 7 and 8.

(☺) Give the children headings such as 'drawing graphs', 'learning about the mode', 'working with a partner' or 'thinking about probability'.

Constructing charts
Classroom technique: Telephone conversation

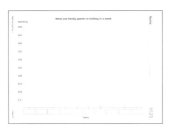

Learning objectives

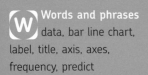

Maths
Discuss a bar line chart showing the frequency of an event

Speaking and listening
'Reach an understanding with your partner'
Reach a common understanding with a partner

Personal skills
'Take pride in your work'
Improve learning and performance: take pride in work

Words and phrases
data, bar line chart, label, title, axis, axes, frequency, predict

Resources
display copy of RS21
for each pair:
copies of RS21
pencils and rulers

Telephone conversation
Children can put a barrier between them or work back to back so that they cannot see each other's work, but can hear each other: "The spending on comics is £12."

Introduction

Pose the scenario that a family is spending a week on holiday at a seaside adventure camp. All the meals and entertainment are paid for. What extra things might the family spend money on during that week? Brainstorm the children's ideas and list these on the board.

> beach toys   drinks   postcards   comics   sunglasses
> sweets   crisps   flip-flops   umbrella   hat

Stop when you have 10 or 12 ideas. Children discuss with their neighbour how much a family might spend on one of these items in a week – such as drinks.

Display RS21. Write in the items from the brainstorm list along the markers on the horizontal axis.

m *How much might you and your family spend on drinks in a week? How do you work it out?*

🗣 *I'm recording a spending of £20 on drinks. Tell me when to stop drawing this bar.*

🗣 *Tell your neighbour two things you would buy if you had £2 to spend, and roughly how much they might cost.*

Pairs

Give each pair of children two copies of RS21 for them to write in the items from the brainstorm on the horizontal axis of the chart.

Children sit so that they cannot see each other's sheet. They take turns to decide on an item and amount, tell their partner of their decision and then both draw in the bar to the correct height.

When they have spent £50 altogether, pairs compare the two charts, checking that they are the same.

m *How do you work out where £7 comes to?*

🗣 *How will you negotiate this? Will Joey ask you for information or will you tell him what you think he needs to know?*

😊 *In what way are you two really good communicators?*

What do you need to do to make sure that you and your partner complete the chart correctly?

Support: Children stick to spending in multiples of £5.

Extend: Children create a chart where the total spending is £100.

Plenary

As a class, discuss and compare the children's completed graphs. Children ask questions about the range of different graphs produced.

(m) *Which item did your family spend most money on?*

(m) *How many people have sweets as the item of highest spending?*

(S) *This pair's family spends £8 on crisps. Does your family spend more or less than that? Tell your partner.*

Assessment for learning

Can the children

(m) Read the total amount of spending on each category from the completed chart?

(S) Work with a partner to check that their two charts match?

(☺) Produce an accurate and legible piece of work?

If not

(m) Make sure that children understand that the value of those bar lines that do not exactly reach a horizontal line can only be estimated.

(S) Ask the class to suggest strategies for sharing out the work fairly. Also keep an eye out on pairs who may not be well matched.

(☺) Remind children to take more time if they need it, rather than hurrying. Check if any of the children have poor motor coordination.

Making charts independently
Classroom technique: Think, pair, share

Learning objectives

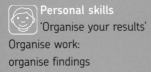

m Maths
Construct
a bar line chart

Speaking and listening
'Join in a discussion with
the whole class'
Contribute to whole-class
discussion

Personal skills
'Organise your results'
Organise work:
organise findings

W Words and phrases
data, database, bar
chart, bar line graph, label,
title, axis, axes, mode,
random, predict

r Resources
piece of shared text
lined or squared paper
and rulers
reading books
or other texts

Think, pair, share
Children think about this for half
a minute alone, then turn to a
partner and share their thoughts
with them. After another
half-minute, the pair share
their ideas with another pair.

Think, pair, share
Children think for two minutes
alone about issues such as:
– the maximum value to put on
  the vertical axis
– what intervals to mark
– how to label the axes
  and graph
They then turn to a partner and
share thoughts with them.
After another few minutes, the
pair share their ideas with the
other pair.

Introduction

Children work in groups of four. Display a piece
of shared text (either projected or in print). Children
look at this briefly and estimate which vowel occurs
most often.

Do a quick count of the vowels as a check.

m *How will you make that estimate? Does it help to
estimate how many times each vowel appears?*

Groups of four

Give each group of children the same copy of a piece
of text. Each child chooses a string of 20 words at
random and makes a simple tally of how often each
vowel appears.

The whole group combine their results.

					Total
a	5	7	5	6	23
e	8	9	10	6	33
i	5	5	3	6	19
o	12	4	3	7	26
u	2	6	2	8	18

Children then think about how to make a bar line graph
or bar graph on plain, lined or squared paper to show
this data.

Each child then makes their own graph, using the
combined group data.

m *What interval are you using? Why is that?*

m *Does it matter what order you put the vowels
in? Why?*

*Tell your partner how you are going to label
your graph, and why.*

*Now you've talked about how to do the graph
together, are you more confident about starting?*

*Does talking together help you get clearer about
what to do?*

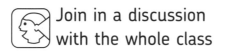
Support: Use 'Peer tutoring' (p8) if children need support to make their graphs.

Extend: Give half the group a text in a different language for them to explore whether the same vowel is most common in both languages.

Plenary

Groups discuss what their graphs tell them.

Discuss the groups' results with the whole class.

Think, pair, share
Use this technique again.

(m) *Was the same vowel the mode for each group? Is that what you expected?*

Tell the class why you think that 'e' is always the most common vowel.

Do you think that if you were to draw your own graphs again, you could do them more quickly and accurately?

Assessment for learning

Can the children	If not
(m) Choose sensible intervals to mark on their vertical axis and ensure that all the data fits?	(m) Look with the class at a successful graph and ask the child who made it to describe the decisions they had to make.
Take turns when talking in pairs and fours?	Ask the group to take responsibility for everyone having a turn to speak – and for listening to each other. Consider using a 'talking stick' (p10).
Make the necessary decisions about the graph they are drawing and justify these?	Give children further opportunities for work that involves decision making, supported by a confident partner. Identify their areas of success and give these positive emphasis.

Name _____

Self and peer assessment

Lesson 17: Exploring probabilities	I think	My partner thinks
(m) I can place the probability of an event on a scale.		
I listen to somebody else's ideas without interrupting.		
I keep trying even when I don't know if my answers are right.		

Lesson 18: Interpreting data	I think	My partner thinks
(m) I can make a prediction about the shape of a graph.		
I can explain why '2' was not likely to be the mode of the graph.		
I can name one thing I have learned in this lesson.		

Name _____

Lesson 19: Constructing charts	I think	My partner thinks
(m) I can record facts on a bar line chart.		
I can work with a partner to check that our two charts match.		
I can produce a piece of work to be proud of.		

Lesson 20: Making charts independently	I think	My partner thinks
(m) I can choose a scale on the vertical axis so that all the data fits.		
I let other people have a turn when we are talking in pairs and fours, and I listen to what they say.		
I make decisions about my work and say why I have made them.		

Self and peer assessment

Listening Chart

Word Bank.

| March | April | May | June |
| September | October | November | December |

Measures

Learning objectives

	Lessons			
	21	22	23	24
ⓜ Maths objectives				
express the formula for the perimeter of a rectangle in words	●			
read clock faces and work out lengths of time		●		
suggest suitable units to estimate or measure length, mass or capacity			●	
express the formula for the area of a rectangle in words				●
Speaking and listening skills				
use precise language to explain ideas or give information	●			
use the processes and language of decision making		●		
contribute to small-group discussion			●	
explain and justify thinking				●
Personal skills				
work with others: work cooperatively with others	●			
improve learning and performance: critically evaluate own work		●		
improve learning and performance: develop confidence in own judgements			●	
organise work: use different approaches to tackle a problem				●

About these lessons

Lesson 21: Measuring perimeters

 Express the formula for the perimeter of a rectangle in words

Children sometimes confuse perimeter and area. This activity asks children to draw a rectangle and to choose what information to give their partner so that they can draw an identical one. In this context, the perimeters of the shapes become important – and the concept of perimeter memorable.

 Use precise language to explain ideas or give information

Classroom technique: Telephone conversation

One child gives information about a rectangle they have drawn to enable their partner who cannot see the original to draw one the same. This focuses children on the language used to describe the dimensions of rectangles.

 Work with others: work cooperatively with others

To use the 'Telephone conversation' technique successfully, children must cooperate, as the technique depends on close communication between each other.

Lesson 22: Time problems

 Read clock faces and work out lengths of time

This activity gives children experience of problem solving with time. Working out time differences can be quite complex. Here, children set some of their own problems and are encouraged to assess their own ability and set problems to match.

 Use the processes and language of decision making

Classroom technique: Heads or tails

In preparation for the plenary, pairs work together and share the decision making and the calculations. This is because they know that if they are invited to the front of the class to explain their ideas, either one of them may be asked to do the talking.

 Improve learning and performance: critically evaluate own work

Children tackle an open-ended problem where they set their own level of difficulty. Discussion and careful questioning can encourage children to think about whether they are setting this work at a level that challenges them appropriately.

Lesson 23: Measuring units

 Suggest suitable units to estimate or measure length, mass or capacity

In this activity, children read statements about measurement and choose which one of the suggested measures is a 'sensible' amount. This helps them develop a 'feel' for units of measure, which is essential for adult life.

 Contribute to small-group discussion

Classroom technique: Think, pair, share

Children consider a problem individually. They then explain their ideas to a partner. After the pair has discussed the issue, they join another pair, share views and emerge with a group conclusion.

 Improve learning and performance: develop confidence in own judgements

Children focus on deciding which measurement and unit are the most likely fit for a 'real-life' context. Thinking about and discussing these measurements gives children a better sense of size and helps them feel confident about their reasons for deciding on the best fit.

Lesson 24: Areas of rectangles

 Express the formula for the area of a rectangle in words

Sometimes, children stick with a trusted but inefficient method, rather than embracing a new one. In this lesson, children try out at least two methods for finding area and are encouraged to practise the one they deem most efficient.

 Explain and justify thinking

Classroom technique: Ticket to explain

When a child wants to explain their method of working to the class, their 'ticket' to be able to do this is to re-explain the method of the child immediately before them. Children hear each method explained twice and have to listen carefully to their peers, rather than simply think about their own method.

Organise work: use different approaches to tackle a problem

The class share methods for finding area, then children try a method that was unfamiliar to them before. This helps them acquire a wider view of what area is all about and to understand that there is more than one way to tackle a problem.

Measuring perimeters

Classroom technique: Telephone conversation

Learning objectives

(m) Maths
Express the formula for the perimeter of a rectangle in words

Speaking and listening
'Use precise language when talking'
Use precise language to explain ideas or give information

Personal skills
'Work cooperatively with others'
Work with others: work cooperatively with others

(W) Words and phrases
length, width, perimeter, measure, dimensions, information, data, calculate, rule, relationship

(r) Resources
for each pair:
centimetre-squared paper
copy of RS22

Perimeter
Remind children that the perimeter is a measure of length – as in a perimeter fence.

Telephone conversation
Children work back to back, leaning their paper on a book, so that they cannot see each other's work, but can hear each other: "The length is 14 cm, and the width is 5 cm. What is the perimeter?"

Squares and rectangles
You may want to remind children that squares are a special kind of rectangle, in which the length and breadth are the same.

Introduction

Practise with the class how to find the perimeter of a rectangle when the length and the width of the rectangle are known.

Establish the formula in words – 'twice the width and twice the length' or 'length plus width times two'.

(m) *Is that the only rectangle with that perimeter? How do you know?*

(speaking) *Tell your partner what two pieces of information you need to find the perimeter of a rectangle.*

Pairs

Give each pair of children a copy of RS22 and two sheets of centimetre-squared paper.

Child A draws a rectangle on squared paper in secret and records three facts about it: the perimeter, length and width. They tell their partner the perimeter and one other fact.

Child B then draws a rectangle of the same dimensions and works out the missing fact. They check this with their partner.

Pairs then record all three facts about their rectangle on RS22.

Children now swap roles and continue until both children have initiated four rectangles.

(m) *Would one piece of information be enough for you to draw the rectangle? Why not?*

(m) *If the rectangle's width and length are the same, what do you know about its shape?*

(speaking) *Talk to your partner about why your rectangles are not the same. Can either of you spot what has gone wrong?*

(personal) *Are you happy with the way you and your partner are working together? Is there anything you want to say to her?*

Support: Children start by providing data about the length and width of the rectangle from which their partner works out the perimeter. Encourage them to move on to giving the perimeter and one other fact.

Extend: Children include some half-centimetres in their dimensions.

Plenary

Tell the class two facts about a rectangle (out of length, breadth and perimeter) and ask them to work out the missing fact with their partner. Include some impossible rectangles (for example, 'perimeter 20 cm and length 12 cm') for children to spot.

(m) *If the rectangle is a square, can you work out the length of the sides from just the perimeter? How?*

(🗣) *Explain to your partner why that rectangle is impossible.*

Assessment for learning

Can the children

(m) Draw a rectangle correctly when given its perimeter and either length or width?

(🗣) Talk with their partner in order to explore and correct any errors?

(🙂) Set work at an appropriate level of challenge for their partner?

If not

(m) Check if children are sure about how to find the perimeter when given the length and width. Model on the board how to use trial and improvement to draw a rectangle when given its perimeter and length.

(🗣) Ask a confident pair of children to demonstrate in front of the class how they deal with the task.

(🙂) Consider whether the pairs are well suited. Ask children to tell their partner what work they think they would find 'quite easy' and then tell them to set work at that level, progressing in stages to more challenging work as appropriate.

Time problems

Classroom technique: Heads or tails

Introduction

Display RS23 and discuss it with the class. Explain that this shows the times of the morning activities at Priory School.

Working together as a class, fill in the times and work out the length of the relevant sessions.

Maths starts 9:10 am   Playtime starts 10:20 am

Maths lasts 1 hour 10 minutes

m *If the minute hand points there, where should the hour hand be?*

m *Is that session more or less than one hour long? Tell your partner how you know that.*

Forming pairs
Put together children of roughly similar abilities so that a problem challenges both.

Self-assessment
Children talk to their partner about what they find straightforward when telling the time and working out time differences – and what they find more difficult.
They use this when setting their own work on RS23, aiming to challenge themselves enough but not too much.

U&A Work methodically to check solutions
With complex problems such as these, children need to check their work. Talk to the class about different ways in which they might do this, but let pairs choose their own method.

Pairs

Give each pair of children a copy of RS23. Pairs work together to plan the morning their way, completing the clock hands and filling the gaps in the corresponding statements.

They then fill in the chart, showing the length of each session.

How did you plan this work? Why did you decide to make the art session that long?

Were any of these calculations easy for you? Too easy? How well did you manage to challenge yourselves?

Support: Suggest that children stick to whole- and half-hour slots for the activities. Provide a geared clock so they can model the passing of time between the beginning and end of sessions.

Extend: Ask children to plan how to spend a whole six-hour day, using RS24.

Plenary

Pairs show the rest of the class how they tackled the activity. Use 'Heads or tails' (p12) to decide which partner will talk about one of the school sessions they planned: its start and end times, and how they worked out its duration.

(m) *Which of these sessions are longer than an hour?*

(☒) *Shall we ask this pair how long they work out the football session to be?*

Heads or tails

Tell children early on in the session that you will be using this technique to ensure they are equally prepared to talk to the class.

Assessment for learning

Can the children

(m) Work out the duration of a session when given the times of its starting and ending?

(☒) Agree timings for the sessions at Priory School?

(☺) Set themselves work that challenges them appropriately?

If not

(m) Practise this skill on a daily basis, using the length of real sessions in school. Use a geared clock to model time passing.

(☒) Discuss ways of doing this fairly – for example, taking turns to choose a time.

(☺) Ask children what would be an easy problem, what would be a harder problem and what they would find manageable but demanding.

Measuring units

Classroom technique: Think, pair, share

Learning objectives

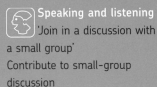

Maths
Suggest suitable units to estimate or measure length, mass or capacity

Speaking and listening
'Join in a discussion with a small group'
Contribute to small-group discussion

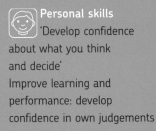

Personal skills
'Develop confidence about what you think and decide'
Improve learning and performance: develop confidence in own judgements

Words and phrases
measure, size, compare, standard unit, guess, close to, about the same as, exact, approximate, estimate

Resources
measuring tools such as rulers, gram weights and litre measures
objects such as a litre carton of juice and a kilogram bag of sugar for each pair;
copy of RS25

U&A Reasoning
Tell children that you will be asking for reasons for their chosen answers.

Estimation
In everyday life, measurement often means estimation and informal comparison: we 'judge' that a kilogram of apples will be enough for the family and 'reckon' that a walk was about 3 km long. Emphasise to children that exact measurement is not always the aim.

Think, pair, share
The procedure is:
– individual considers questions
– pair shares thoughts
– two pairs join together and aim to reach consensus

Peer tutoring
This has similarities with 'Peer tutoring' (p8). Children with a good feel for the size of a unit help their peer(s) acquire the same understanding.

Introduction

Look with the class at a range of measuring tools such as rulers, gram weights and litre measures and discuss the size of the units measured. This will give children benchmarks as a basis for their imaginings and discussions.

m *Take turns with your partner to say something you might measure in litres.*

Why would it be difficult to measure the distance from here to London in millimetres?

Groups of four

Children work in pairs, with a copy of RS25 each. Individuals read the questions and think about them on their own, then discuss with their partner how to answer each question and reach agreement where possible.

Each pair then joins with another pair and compares their work, making a note of any questions that they have answered differently. They discuss these questions, aiming to reach consensus.

m *Remember the metre stick? Show me a metre with your hands. So how long is 2 metres?*

m *Can you think of something that weighs about a kilogram?*

Explain to Maya why you think the answer is 'more than 20 metres'.

Check your answers and see if there are any you are unsure about. Ask the other pair about them.

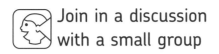
Support: Provide objects whose measurements are known to give children a 'base line' for their comparisons: a centimetre ruler, a kilogram of sugar or a litre of juice.

Extend: Pairs write their own questions on the bottom of RS25 for their partner pair to tackle.

Plenary

1, 2, 3, 4
Number the children 1, 2, 3 and 4. Roll a dice to determine which of them answers your question (roll again if you get 5 or 6).

Choose one of the groups of four. Read out one of the questions and ask one of them to answer it, giving their reasons.

Repeat this process with other groups and other questions.

🅜 *How many metres long do you reckon this classroom is?*

🗨 *Explain why you gave the answer as '30 grams'.*

☺ *You seem certain about that answer. Tell me why.*

Assessment for learning

Can the children

🅜 Make appropriate estimates about the measures and units in the problems?

🗨 Take part in the discussion when pairs join up?

☺ Talk about when and why they are sure of an answer – and when they are not?

If not

🅜 Establish which particular measures and units children have problems with and do further practical work involving these.

🗨 Consider introducing 'talking sticks' (p10) – decorated sticks that confer on the holder the right and responsibility to speak and be listened to.

☺ Work to create a classroom climate where uncertainty is accepted and where 'having a go' is valued, so that children don't need to fear criticism if they 'get it wrong'.

Areas of rectangles

Classroom technique: Ticket to explain

Learning objectives

(m) Maths
Express the formula for the area of a rectangle in words

(speaking) Speaking and listening
'Explain what you think and why you think it'
Explain and justify thinking

(personal) Personal skills
'Try different ways to tackle a problem'
Organise work: use different approaches to tackle a problem

(W) Words and phrases
area, covers, surface, square centimetre, method, measure, quick, accurate, efficient

(r) Resources
a leaf from a tree
a sheet of paper
for each pair:
copy of RS26

How to find areas
Don't actually discuss at this stage how to find areas in order to avoid pre-empting the later discussion of this.

Different methods
Some children may sketch in the 'hidden' squares, then count each square in the rectangle. Others may use a more sophisticated method. At this stage of the lesson, give equal value to all methods that work.

Introduction

Show the class a leaf, a sheet of paper and the palm of your hand. Use them to revise the difference between area and perimeter.

(speaking) *Talk with your partner. Try to reach a definition of what 'area' means.*

Pairs

Give each pair of children a copy of RS26. Pairs work together to find and record the area of rectangles A, B and C. They also need to talk through how they have done it, in case they are called on to explain to the class.

A

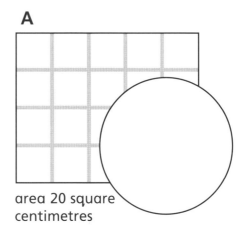

area 20 square centimetres

Hold a class discussion about children's different methods, using 'Ticket to explain' (p11).

Children return to RS26 and tackle the next three rectangles, using a different method to the first one, even if it seems more cumbersome to them.

Children then find the areas of the last three rectangles, using the most efficient method.

(m) *Tell us how you found the area of that rectangle.*

(m) *Tell me Billy's method for finding the area.*

(speaking) *Suppose the entire end of the rectangle was covered. Could you find the area then? Why not?*

Support: Help children count the squares in fives, fours or whatever multiple is appropriate, rather than counting each square.

Extend: Ask children how much of a rectangle can be covered and the area still be found. Ask them to find a formula in symbols for the area of a rectangle.

Plenary

Using 'Ticket to explain' again, ask a few children which method they now prefer and whether this has changed in the course of the lesson.

(m) *What do you need to know to find the area of a rectangle?*

(☺) *Which method do you prefer? And why?*

(☺) *Is the method you like best also the quickest?*

Ticket to explain
Warn children in good time that you are going to use this technique and remind them to listen carefully to the explanations given by other children.

Assessment for learning

Can the children

(m) Find the area of a part-hidden rectangle?

If not

(m) Help the children count the squares in equal jumps: "5, 10, 15, 20 squares."

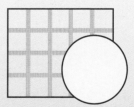

(👤) Explain why they favour a particular method?

(👤) Give children hints: was one method quicker or more reliable? Were they more confident about the accuracy of one method?

(☺) Understand and use a method that is new to them?

(☺) Rearrange pairs so that children who favour different methods work together, demonstrating their method to their partner.

Name _____

Self and peer assessment

Lesson 21: Measuring perimeters	I think	My partner thinks
(m) I can draw a rectangle correctly if I know its perimeter and either its length or its width.		
I work out with my partner the errors that either of us has made.		
I set work for my partner that is not too hard and not too easy.		

Lesson 22: Time problems	I think	My partner thinks
(m) I can work out the length of a session when given the times of its starting and ending.		
I agree with my partner the times to put on the clocks.		
I invent problems that are neither too easy nor too hard.		

Name _____

Self and peer assessment

Lesson 23: Measuring units	I think	My partner thinks
(m) I can use estimation to find the correct answers to problems.		
I listen to others when they talk about their ideas.		
I can say when I am sure of an answer – and when I am not.		

Lesson 24: Areas of rectangles	I think	My partner thinks
(m) I can find the area of a rectangle by counting squares when part of it is hidden.		
I can explain why I like to use the method I do.		
I can learn to use a different method, even if I don't like it.		

Listening Chart

Word Bank.

March   April   May   June

September   October   November   December

Shape and space

Learning objectives

	Lessons			
	25	**26**	**27**	**28**
ⓜ Maths objectives				
identify nets of a cube	●			
describe 2D shapes		●		
recognise properties of rectangles			●	
carry out a mathematical investigation				●
Ⓢ Speaking and listening skills				
reach a common understanding with a partner	●			
explain and justify thinking		●		
share and discuss ideas and reach consensus			●	
contribute to whole-class discussion				●
Ⓢ Personal skills				
work with others: overcome difficulties and recover from mistakes	●			
improve learning and performance: take pride in work		●		
organise work: plan and manage a group task			●	
improve learning and performance: assess learning progress				●

About these lessons

Lesson 25: Nets of cubes

 Identify nets of a cube

This activity requires children to relate 3D solids and 2D shapes in two ways: they think about which nets will fold up into cubes and also think about which faces will then be opposite each other.

 Reach a common understanding with a partner

Classroom technique: One between two

Children take turns to be 'Instructor' or 'Net Drawer'. The Instructor works out what to do and tells their partner what to record with the pencil. Having just one pencil per pair encourages children to communicate well, as they are dependent on each other to complete the task.

 Work with others: overcome difficulties and recover from mistakes

Children make nets of cubes and check that they work. If a net doesn't work, they can find a way to adapt it so that it does, learning in the process that errors are simply a step on the way to getting something right.

Lesson 26: Reasoning about shapes

 Describe 2D shapes

This activity requires children to think carefully about the properties of shapes, examining each property in turn and considering whether it does, or does not, describe their given shape.

 Explain and justify thinking

Classroom technique: Tell your partner

Children put their thoughts into words as they explain to their partner why they think a particular description does, or does not, fit a shape.

 Improve learning and performance: take pride in work

Carrying out mathematical investigations allows children to set their own goals and offers flexibility about how they approach their work. This open-ended situation provides a rich context in which to encourage children to take pride in their work.

Lesson 27: Properties of rectangles

 Recognise properties of rectangles

Although children may be able to recognise rectangles intuitively, they may not be sure about their properties. This activity encourages children to discuss statements about rectangles to refine their understanding and expand their vocabulary.

 Share and discuss ideas and reach consensus

Classroom technique: Rotating roles

This technique ensures equal participation by each member of the group. One child is the 'Chairperson' and allows everyone a chance to say what they think. Another is the 'Recorder' and records the consensus. These roles change with each problem.

Organise work: plan and manage a group task

The task is initially structured, but then becomes more open as the group prepares a presentation on rectangles for the class. Children benefit from the experience of working in both a structured way, when they acquire ideas about group organisation, and in an unstructured way, when they test out these ideas and make them their own.

Lesson 28: Investigating shapes

 Carry out a mathematical investigation

Mathematical investigation is a more open-ended process than problem solving and can be daunting unless the activity is structured. That is precisely what this lesson provides. Its structure could be used for investigations with other mathematical content.

Contribute to whole-class discussion

Classroom technique: Talking partners

This informal partnership allows children to develop and practise the skills of collaboration in unstructured situations. Pairs talk together about the task in hand and about how to present their findings to the class.

Improve learning and performance: assess learning progress

Children tackle an open-ended problem, where they set their own level of difficulty. In the plenary session, they complete an evaluation questionnaire in discussion with a partner, which provides a safe structure in which to assess their own progress in learning.

Nets of cubes

Classroom technique: One between two

Learning objectives

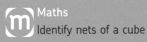 **Maths**
Identify nets of a cube

Speaking and listening
'Reach an understanding with your partner'
Reach a common understanding with a partner

Personal skills
'Get over difficulties and mistakes'
Work with others: overcome difficulties and recover from mistakes

Words and phrases
net, plan, square, cube, face, 2D, two-dimensional, 3D, three-dimensional, position, grid, row, column, horizontal, vertical

Resources
display copy of RS27
for each pair:
two or more copies of RS27
pens or pencils
scissors

Using grid references
If necessary, revise with children how to identify squares on a grid.

One between two
Remind children of the ground rules: communication must be done through speech, not pointing. Only the Net Drawer is allowed to touch the pencil until they swap roles.

Visualisation
Encourage children to try to picture in their heads the 3D shapes that their nets will make.

Introduction

Ask for a volunteer to help you demonstrate the main activity, using 'One between two' (p8). Display RS27 to the class and instruct the child which squares to mark to form the net of a cube. Give the grid reference: "C3 is the base..."

Work out which pairs of squares will be opposite each other and instruct the child to mark these pairs, each in a different way.

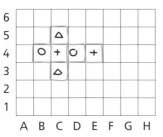

Then reverse roles so that the child tells you a net to draw and how to mark opposite faces.

(m) *If that square is the base of a box, which squares will form the sides of the box? And which one is the lid?*

Pairs

Pairs of children repeat this activity, taking turns to be the 'Instructor' and the 'Net Drawer'.

Pairs work together to check whether (a) they both form cubes, and (b) the opposite faces are as predicted. They can cut out the net if they are not sure.

The children then repeat this exercise to make two more different nets.

(m) *Shut your eyes and imagine a cube. Can you count its faces?*

(m) *Show me how this shape will look when it is folded.*

Do you agree with what Samira is saying about those faces? Why not?

You found out that that net doesn't work. How can you adapt it so that it does make a cube? Can you see what you need to change?

Support: Children make the nets with Polydron or Clixi first, then draw them out on the grid.

Extend: Children try to find all the arrangements of six squares that *don't* make the net of a cube.

Plenary

Display RS27 to the class. Individuals describe a successful net for you to record on the grid, each one different from the last, or sketch the nets on a large sheet of paper.

Leave children to think about any nets they have missed as a 'chewing the fat' exercise (p13). They can add to the collection on the display each day as they think of more.

(m) *Could two squares that are next to each other on this grid ever make the opposite faces of a cube? Why do you think that?*

Chewing the fat

This lesson ends with a challenge for children to ponder in their own time. If you want to pick it up again, and children want hints, suggest they start with four squares in a line and try moving the other squares round this base, then moving on to three squares, and so on.

Here are all 11 possible nets:

Assessment for learning

Can the children

(m) Recognise arrangements of squares that form the net of a cube – and those that don't?

(☒) Convey to a partner how to draw the net they want?

(☺) Find a way to correct any nets they make that don't 'work'?

If not

(m) Provide experience of making cubes from squared paper. Give children some old cereal boxes (cuboids) to cut up and ask them to record the different nets they can make from these.

(☒) Give children square tiles or interlocking flat shapes to plan their net. Suggest that they instruct their partner to mark all six squares before attempting to draw round any of them.

(☺) Suggest that children fold up their net and cut off any overlapping squares, then see where a square is 'missing' and stick it on,s using tape.

Reasoning about shapes
Classroom technique: Tell your partner

Learning objectives

Maths
Describe 2D shapes

Speaking and listening
'Explain what you think and why you think it'
Explain and justify thinking

Personal skills
'Take pride in your work'
Improve learning and performance: take pride in work

Words and phrases
acute, obtuse, table, semicircle, convex, concave, regular, isosceles, scalene, heptagon, pentagon, polygon right-angled, vertex, vertices

Resources
display copy
of RS28
for each pair:
copy of RS28
plastic shapes or cards
cut from RS29 and RS30
mathematical
dictionaries

Tell your partner
Give children a few moments before they hold up their shape to 'tell their partner' (p10) why they think that description does or doesn't fit: "My shape has two acute angles, here and here" or "This isn't a hexagon because it hasn't got six sides."

Tell your partner
Children take turns to write a statement or note about the shape, each time justifying this statement to their partner: "It's irregular, because the sides are different lengths."

Presenting the profile
Remind children to use negative as well as positive statements: "This shape is not convex."

Introduction

Children work in pairs. Display RS28. Give each pair a flat plastic shape (or a card cut from RS29 and RS30). Read out descriptions from RS28 and ask pairs to hold up their shape if it fits that description.

(m) *Hold up all shapes with parallel sides. Does everyone agree that these have parallel sides? Now keep holding up your shape only if it has parallel sides and is a hexagon.*

(m) *Can a shape be a pentagon and a polygon? Why?*

Pairs

Give each pair of children a copy of RS28.

Children use the descriptions as well as their own descriptions to write a profile of their shape.

They then work together to present this profile on a sheet of A4 paper.

This shape
is a 2D shape
has 8 obtuse angles
has straight sides
is convex
is an octagon
has parallel sides
is symmetrical
is a polygon
is regular
has 8 vertices

(m) *Which words or phrases here do not describe your shape?*

(m) *If there aren't many labels that fit your shape, describe it in terms of negatives: "It is not a square."*

(speaking) *Show me a word or phrase here that describes your shape. Justify your choice.*

(personal) *Does the order of your statements matter at all? Why is that?*

Will your profile fit any other shapes as well as yours? Can you write it so as to be sure it doesn't?

Support: Use the same shape for the introduction and the main activity and circle just a few of the descriptions for children to focus on. Talk with children about how to present their work – for example, they could draw round their shape and stick the appropriate statements around it.

Extend: Children select a few descriptions and draw a shape to fit.

Plenary

Display several of the children's shapes. Read out one of the children's profiles, without indicating which shape it describes. Children tell their partner which of the shapes they think is being described.

This profile describes a symmetrical triangle with straight sides and no right angle. Which triangle could it be? Which shapes can't it be? Why?

I know someone who says that polygons are shapes with eight sides, because 'poly' means 'eight'. What do you think? (See 'Devil's advocate', p11.)

Who's got something to show us that you're really pleased with?

Assessment for learning

Can the children

Use a wide range of words and phrases to describe their shape?

Tell their partner why they think a particular description does or does not fit their shape?

Organise their shape profile coherently and neatly?

If not

Ask children to invent a team quiz using words from a maths dictionary or shape vocabulary list.

Provide practice in sorting shapes by using a sorting tree or Carroll diagram and focusing on one property of a shape at a time, as children may lack understanding of the terms used.

Ask children to look at how others in the class are presenting their work and to assess which methods would work well for them and the reader.

Properties of rectangles
Classroom technique: Rotating roles

Learning objectives

(m) Maths
Recognise properties of rectangles

Speaking and listening
'Share ideas and reach agreement as a group'
Share and discuss ideas and reach consensus

Personal skills
'Plan and manage a group task'
Organise work: plan and manage a group task over time

(W) Words and phrases
square, rectangle, oblong, polygon, quadrilateral, vertex, vertices, diagonal, parallel, perpendicular, right angle

(r) Resources
display copy of RS31
for each group:
cards cut from RS31

Thumbs up, thumbs down
This allows you to make an initial assessment of the class's understanding of the issues. Use the plenary to check whether or not children have shifted in their views.

Rotating roles
The 'Chairperson' makes sure that everyone has a chance to say what they think and encourages consensus. The role should rotate round the group after each statement has been dealt with.

Lucky dip
To identify a spokesperson, you or the group choose a name at random. The whole group takes responsibility for briefing this person to present their ideas in the plenary session. Make the selection early enough in the session to allow time for briefing, preparation and, if necessary, rehearsal.

U&A Investigate or test general statements
In this activity, children work with general statements about rectangles, a process that will refine their understanding of the class of quadrilaterals.

Introduction

Display RS31 to the class and slowly read out the statements. Children give a 'thumbs up' or 'thumbs down' to each one to show whether or not they agree with it. (Don't comment on their responses yet.)

Groups of four

Children work in groups of four. Give each group a set of statement cards cut from RS31. Children take each card in turn, discuss it and agree where to put it in 'Yes', 'No' or 'Not sure' piles.

Ask each group to choose the statement about which they had the most discussion and to prepare a presentation for the class, explaining the issues they had with it.

(m) *Tell me some qualities of a rectangle – and some qualities that a rectangle does not have.*

(speaking) *Tell Marie why you are so sure that statement is not true.*

(personal) *What do you do if somebody doesn't agree with where you put a card?*

(personal) *How have you chosen and briefed your spokesperson?*

Support: An available adult works with children who need help discussing the statements. Otherwise, form groups of mixed ability.

Extend: Groups write a 'true' and a 'false' statement about rectangles – and a dubious one, if they can – to discuss in the plenary.

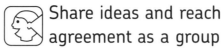
Plenary

Each group makes its presentation (allow no discussion until all groups have spoken).

Hold a class discussion in which the class establishes the status of each statement card.

Stick the statement cards up on a large sheet of paper where all children can see them. Leave them on display after the lesson (see 'Ideas board', p13).

(m) *Could we test whether that statement is true by drawing one or more rectangles?*

Class record

Make alterations to the statement cards so that they all fit into the 'Yes' or 'No' categories.

Yes

Rectangles have four corners.

In rectangles, ~~one pair~~ both pairs of opposite sides ~~is~~ are parallel.

No

Rectangles are not polygons.

Assessment for learning

Can the children

(m) Recognise both a true and a false statement about rectangles?

(s) Explain to the group why they think a statement belongs in the 'Yes' pile?

(☺) Take the role of Chairperson successfully, allowing all other children to be heard?

If not

(m) Try sorting quadrilaterals, including rectangles, onto a Venn diagram, using various criteria.

(s) Ask a confident child to offer this explanation (perhaps in the plenary) and invite children to repeat this to their neighbours.

(☺) Make sure that children are listened to in class properly and model good listening behaviour themselves. If a child lacks authority in the group, remind the other children that the role of Chairperson confers authority to the holder for as long as they are Chair.

Investigating shapes
Classroom technique: Talking partners

Learning objectives

Maths
Carry out a mathematical investigation

Speaking and listening
'Join in a discussion with the whole class'
Contribute to whole-class discussion

Personal skills
'Assess your progress in learning'
Improve learning and performance: assess learning progress

Words and phrases
diagonal, vertex, vertices, congruent, regular, irregular, equilateral, isosceles, scalene, right-angled, pentagon

Resources
display copies of RS32, RS33 and RS34
for each pair:
copies of RS32
pencils and rulers
plain paper
squared paper
dotted paper
scissors
coloured pens or pencils

Definition
Establish that a diagonal of any polygon is a straight line drawn from any vertex to another vertex that is not adjacent.

Talking partners
For this lesson, put together pairs who are familiar partners and have the mutual trust needed to tackle the investigation.

'What I notice'
Children take turns to say a sentence starting with 'What I notice about ...'.

Make some suggestions about what to look for: the number of diagonals, the patterns made, the numbers of triangles, and so on.

Asking questions
Show children how to change one aspect of a question as a way of thinking up a new question.

How many diagonals do *pentagons* have? → How many diagonals do *hexagons* have? Are all the diagonals the same length? → When are all the diagonals the same length?

Presentations
Discuss questions such as:
– Is it a good idea to work in rough first?
– Will they write prose, or draw diagrams, or both?
– What instruments or tools do they need to produce clear diagrams?

Introduction

Display RS32 to the class and work with the children to draw in the diagonals on one of the pentagons.

Children then work in pairs to fill in the diagonals for all the pentagons on their own copies of RS32.

They tell their partner anything they notice about the shapes as they now appear. Collect a few of the children's ideas on the board.

Display RS33 and read through the questions with the class. Add further questions that children might ask about these or other shapes to the sheet.

There are five triangles like this, and the whole shape has five sides. What other relationships can you see?

Tell us why you think there can't be an external diagonal on this pentagon.

Pairs

Pairs choose more questions to explore and answer.

After about ten minutes, stop the class and talk with the children about how to present their work to the class.

You have noticed that the diagonals make a small pentagon in the middle of the big regular pentagon. What do you think happens with a different regular shape – for example, a hexagon? Does it happen with all regular shapes?

Tell your partner why you want to look at the different triangles in the diagrams.

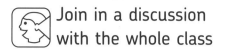
Support: Direct children to the first two questions on RS33.

Extend: Urge children to think about why they get the answers they do – for example, why do all pentagons have five diagonals? Ask for further predictions – for example, if all five-sided shapes have five diagonals, how many diagonals will six- and seven-sided shapes have?

Reframing

When children are trying to express a new idea, you can sometimes help them by rephrasing or 'reframing' it, using different language (see p14): "Sam said those triangles are the same, but pointing different ways. If we rotated this one, we'd get this triangle, then this one, then this one."

Critical evaluation

Children work with new partners, rather than the person they did the grids with. Give them two minutes each to tell their partner the answers to the questions.

Plenary

A few pairs present and talk about their work to the whole class. Choose one or two questions that were tackled widely, as well as one or two that were less frequently chosen.

Display RS34 and read through the questions to the class. Pairs join up and use these questions to do a critical evaluation of their profile, with the other pair as audience.

Other pairs pin up their work on an 'Ideas board' (p13) where the class can see it over the next few days.

(m) *You found out that only a regular pentagon has diagonals that are all the same length. Could that be true of hexagons, too?*

(☺) *What things have you been practising or learning today?*

Assessment for learning

Can the children

(m) Identify a question to tackle and decide how to approach answering it?

(☒) Offer an idea or comment when working in pairs? With the whole class?

(☺) Find something to say about what they have learned during the lesson?

If not

(m) Narrow down the choice for them so that they only have two or three questions to choose from.

(☒) Provide a topic that is open to comment, such as "Tell us something about the number of diagonals you drew" or "What can you say about the triangles in that shape?"

(☺) Offer useful headings such as 'learning to think up my own questions', 'recognising different kinds of triangle', 'working with a partner' or 'presenting my work on paper'.

Self and peer assessment

Lesson 25: Nets of cubes	I think	My partner thinks
(m) I can make a net of a cube.		
I tell my partner which squares to draw round to make a net.		
I am proud of the work I have done with my partner.		

Lesson 26: Reasoning about shapes	I think	My partner thinks
(m) I can describe a shape using at least eight different properties.		
I can explain why I think a description doesn't fit a shape.		
I present my work so that other people can understand it.		

Name _____

Lesson 27: Properties of rectangles	I think	My partner thinks
(m) I know several ways in which rectangles are different from hexagons or triangles.		
I tell my group when I don't agree with someone else's view.		
I help my group to do our task.		

Lesson 28: Investigating shapes	I think	My partner thinks
(m) I can find a way to answer the question that I have chosen.		
I can talk about my work in front of the whole class.		
I can say one thing that I have learned about today.		

Resource sheets

Name _____ RS1

Operations

−0.5   −2   −5   −9

+0.3   +3   +1.5

+15   +10

Starting numbers

0   10

0.14   2.5

1   5   10   25

99   100   500

Maths Out Loud *Year 5*   Lesson 1

Name _____ RS2

0	1	2	3	4
5	6	7	8	9
0	1	2	3	4
5	6	7	8	9
•				

Maths Out Loud *Year 5*   Lesson 2

Name _____ RS3

Number Maker

You have two sets of digit cards.
Arrange some of these to make a
number less than a million.

When you have all finished with this
number, pass this label to the person on
your **left**.

Reader

Look at the number the Number Maker
has made and read it out.

When you have all finished with that
number, pass this label to the person on
your **left**.

Calculator Holder

Listen to the number that the Reader
says. Key that number into the calculator.
You may not look at the digit cards.

When you have all finished with the
number, pass this label to the person on
your **left**.

- Cut out these role labels and fold
  them in half so they stand up.

- Give one of each label to each
  group of three.

- The children can use them to
  identify who is in which role,
  then pass them on after they
  have dealt with each number.

Maths Out Loud *Year 5*   Lesson 2

Name _____ RS4

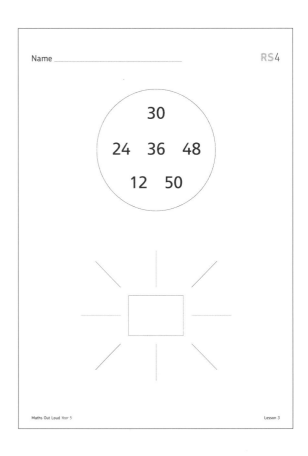

Maths Out Loud *Year 5*   Lesson 3

RS5

Name _____

Improper fractions

A $3\frac{1}{4}$ (three and a quarter)
is an improper fraction.

B $\frac{4.5}{12}$ (four point five over twelve)
is an improper fraction.

C $\frac{896}{12}$ (eight hundred and ninety-six
over twelve) is an improper fraction.

Percentages

A 33% (thirty-three per cent) is the same
as $\frac{330}{1000}$ (three hundred and thirty over
one thousand).

B 33% (thirty-three per cent) is the same
as 3.3 (three point three).

C 33% (thirty-three per cent) is the same
as $\frac{3}{10}$ (three tenths).

RS6

Name _____

Decimals

A 0.5 (zero point five) metres is less than
0.41 (zero point four one) metres.

B 0.53 (zero point five three) is greater
than 0.4 (zero point four).

C 0.09 (zero point zero nine) is greater
than 0.2 (zero point two).

Size of fractions

A If you cut something into six pieces,
each piece must be one sixth.

B $\frac{1}{6}$ (one sixth) can be bigger
than $\frac{1}{2}$ (one half).

C $\frac{1}{6}$ (one sixth) of something can never
be a whole number.

RS7

Name _____

$\frac{1}{2}$	$\frac{1}{2}$
$\frac{1}{4}$	$\frac{1}{4}$
$\frac{3}{4}$	$\frac{3}{4}$
$\frac{1}{10}$	$\frac{1}{10}$
$\frac{2}{10}$	$\frac{2}{10}$
$\frac{3}{10}$	$\frac{3}{10}$
$\frac{7}{10}$	$\frac{7}{10}$
$\frac{9}{10}$	$\frac{9}{10}$

RS8

Name _____

1st board

50%	10%	75%	20%
75%	25%	50%	90%
30%	20%	30%	25%
70%	90%	10%	70%

2nd board

5%	15%	60%	40%
75%	80%	10%	12%
33%	23%	95%	30%
2%	1%	14%	99%

RS9

Name _____

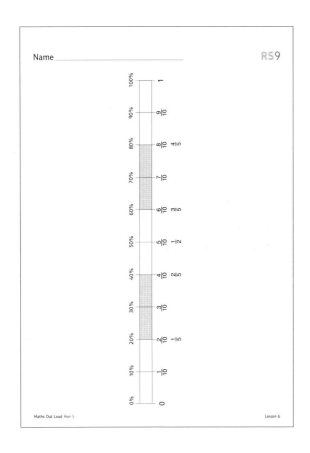

RS10

Name _____

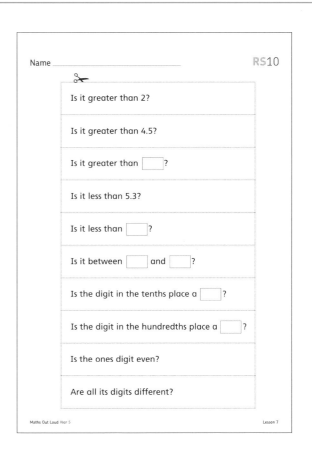

Is it greater than 2?

Is it greater than 4.5?

Is it greater than ☐?

Is it less than 5.3?

Is it less than ☐?

Is it between ☐ and ☐?

Is the digit in the tenths place a ☐?

Is the digit in the hundredths place a ☐?

Is the ones digit even?

Are all its digits different?

RS11

Name _____

Dice numbers	Calculation

A _____ ☐☐ − ☐☐ = ◯

B _____ ☐☐ − ☐☐ = ◯

C _____ ☐☐☐ + ☐☐ = ◯

D _____ ☐☐☐ + ☐☐ = ◯

E _____ ☐☐☐ − ◯ = ☐☐

F _____ ☐☐ + ◯ = ☐☐☐

G _____ ☐.☐ + ◯ = ☐

H _____ 0.☐ + ◯ = ☐.☐

I _____ ☐☐ × **2** = ◯

J _____ ☐.☐ × **2** = ◯

K _____ ◯ × **2** = ☐☐☐

L _____ ◯ − ◯ = ☐☐☐

RS12

Name _____

Game 1

Number made with dice		+ or –?	Total so far
			50
1			
2			
3			
4			
5			
6			
7			
8			
9			
10			
11			
12			
13			
14			
15			
16			

The winners are: ....

Game 2

Number made with dice		+ or –?	Total so far
			50
1			
2			
3			
4			
5			
6			
7			
8			
9			
10			
11			
12			
13			
14			
15			
16			

The winners are: ....

RS13

Name _____

Elmridge School Outing

You are members of Elmridge School Council. The School Council is putting together a proposal for an outing to the seaside for the whole school. The journey from the school to the seaside takes half an hour.

The headteacher wants the proposal to include:
• the number of coaches needed
• how many adults will go with the children
• the total cost of the outing

Please prepare your proposal.

School classes

Class	1	2	3	4	5	6
Pupils	27	32	33	28	34	31

Outings policy
One adult to accompany each group of ten children.
All children to bring packed lunches.

Classy Coaches

Charge sheet

£250 per day (8 hours)
£150 per half day
(any 5 hours after 10:00 am)
Note: Each coach seats 53 people

RS14

Name _____

number	equal to
lots of	calculate
groups of	work out
times	solve
product	question
multiply	answer
multiplied by	same number
multiplication facts	number line
multiplication tables	multiplication grid
multiple	counters
factor	cubes
add	division
repeated addition	inverse
array	number
double	count
how many ...?	

RS15

Name _____

1	2	3	4	5	6	7	8	9	10
2	4	6	8	10	12	14	16	18	20
3	6	9	12	15	18	21	24	27	30
4	8	12	16	20	24	28	32	36	40
5	10	15	20	25	30	35	40	45	50
6	12	18	24	30	36	42	48	54	60
7	14	21	28	35	42	49	56	63	70
8	16	24	32	40	48	56	64	72	80
9	18	27	36	45	54	63	72	81	90
10	20	30	40	50	60	70	80	90	100

RS16

Name _____

Word problems

$129 \div 6 = 21 \text{ r } 3$	$129 \div 6 = 21.5$	$129 \div 6 = 21\frac{1}{2} \text{ or } 21\frac{1}{2}$

1 A farmer collects 129 eggs to take to the farmers' market.
She packs them into boxes, 6 at a time.
How many full egg boxes can she take to sell?

	Answer	Reason
A	22 boxes	because you need a spare box for the 3 extra eggs
B	21.5 boxes	because 21.5 is the answer to 129 ÷ 6
C	21 boxes	because she fills only 21 boxes and there will be 3 eggs over
D	21½ boxes	because you can fill 21 and a half boxes

2 A school takes 129 children camping. Each tent sleeps 6 children.
How many tents do they take for the children?

	Answer	Reason
A	21 tents	because you can fill 21 tents and there are 3 people left over
B	22 tents	because you need 22 tents to sleep everyone
C	21½ tents	because you need half a tent for the people left over
D	21.5 tents	because 129 divided by 6 is 21.5

3 129 metres of silk is shared equally between 6 tailors.
How much silk does each tailor get?

	Answer	Reason
A	22 metres	because they will all get nearly 22 metres
B	21½ metres	because you get 6 lengths of 21½ metres from 129 metres
C	21 metres	because each tailor gets 21 metres, with 3 metres spare
D	22 metres	because you round up 21.5 metres to 22 metres

4 6 adults travel to Solihull on the train. The cost of the six tickets is £129.
How much is each ticket?

	Answer	Reason
A	£22	because you round up the answer to a whole number of pounds
B	£21.50	because 6 lots of £21.50 is £129
C	21½	because 21½ is what you get when you divide £129 by 6
D	£21	because there are 6 lots of £21 in £129, with some left over

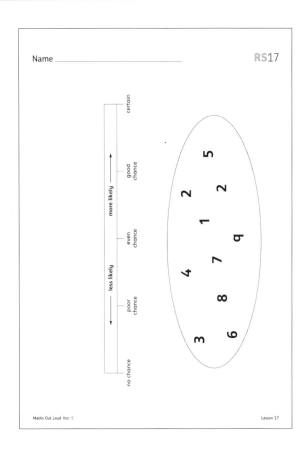

Name _____ RS17

Name _____ RS18

A   I'll have a birthday in the next month.

B   I will be 12 on my next birthday.

C   I'll enjoy my dinner today.

D   It will rain tonight.

E   It will snow tomorrow.

F   The next school I go to will be …

G   I will live to be 100.

H   A unicorn will walk through the room soon.

I   I will be a deep-sea diver when I grow up.

J   _____

K   _____

L   _____

(Write your own statements for J, K and L.)

no chance   poor chance   even chance   good chance   certain

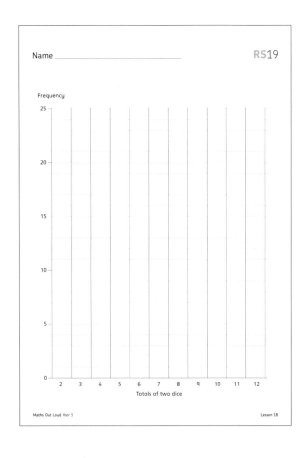

Name _____ RS19

Frequency

Totals of two dice

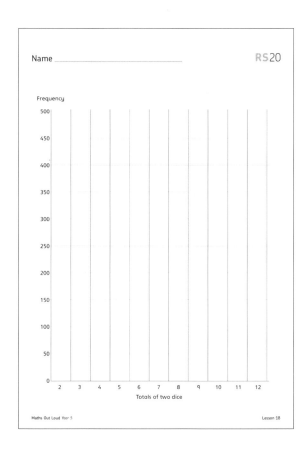

Name _____ RS20

Frequency

Totals of two dice

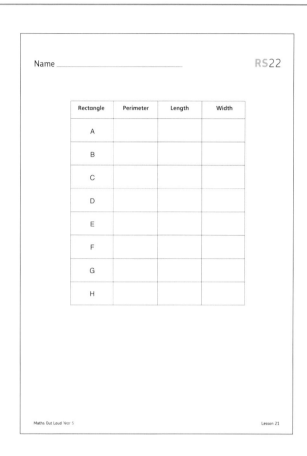

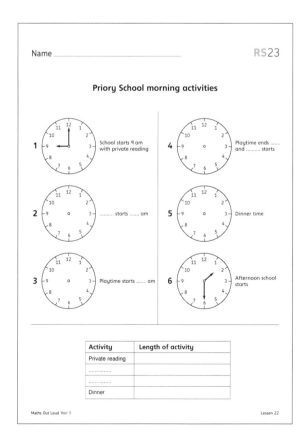

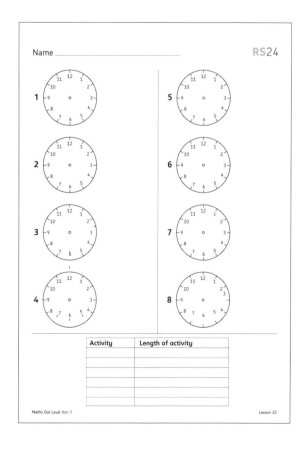

Sheet RS21

Name _____ RS21

What one family spends on holiday in a week

Spending: £50, £45, £40, £35, £30, £25, £20, £15, £10, £5

Items

Sheet RS22

Name _____ RS22

Rectangle	Perimeter	Length	Width
A			
B			
C			
D			
E			
F			
G			
H			

Sheet RS23

Name _____ RS23

Priory School morning activities

1. School starts 9 am with private reading
2. .... starts .... am
3. Playtime starts .... am
4. Playtime ends .... and .... starts
5. Dinner time
6. Afternoon school starts

Activity	Length of activity
Private reading	
....	
....	
Dinner	

Sheet RS24

Name _____ RS24

1   5
2   6
3   7
4   8

Activity	Length of activity

Name _____ RS25

What do you think?

1. A postcard weighs about **500 kg, 900 g** or **40 g**.

2. The thickness of a postcard is **more** or **less** than 1 millimetre.

3. In a week, I drink about **2 litres** or **2 millilitres** of milk.

4. A garden fence is about **2 metres, 10 metres** or **100 metres** high.

5. A giant's pencil might be about **50 cm, 5 m** or **5 kilometres** long.

6. A plum weighs about **30 grams, 300 grams** or **3000 grams**.

7. A coach journey from London to Edinburgh takes **30 minutes, 8 hours** or **3 days**.

8. The perimeter of the classroom is **more** or **less** than 20 metres.

9. I can walk one kilometre in **20 minutes** or **20 seconds**.

What do you think?

1.

2.

3.

4.

5.

Maths Out Loud Year 5   Lesson 23

Name _____ RS26

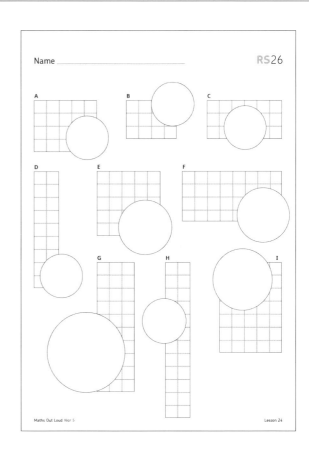

Maths Out Loud Year 5   Lesson 24

Name _____ RS27

Maths Out Loud Year 5   Lesson 25

Name _____ RS28

2D shape	octagon
has an acute angle	has parallel sides
has an obtuse angle	pentagon
has a curved side	symmetrical
circle	polygon
has straight sides	quadrilateral
convex	triangle
concave	rectangle
equilateral triangle	regular
hexagon	has a right angle
heptagon	right-angled triangle
irregular	scalene triangle
isosceles triangle	semicircle
oblong	square

Maths Out Loud Year 5   Lesson 26

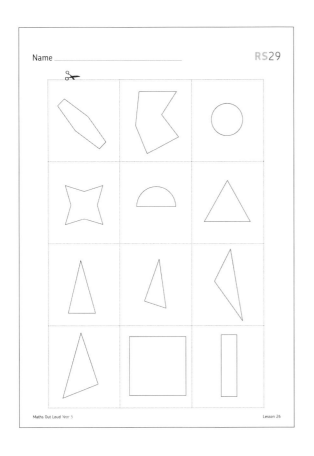

Name _____ RS29

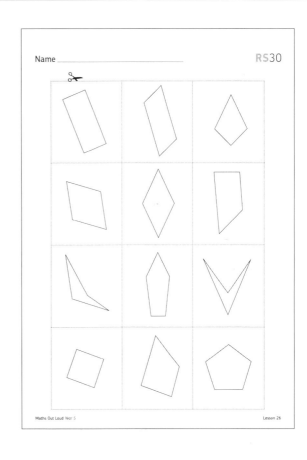

Name _____ RS30

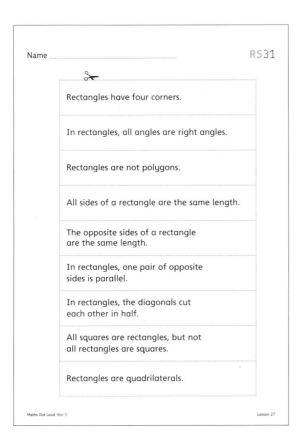

Name _____ RS31

Rectangles have four corners.

In rectangles, all angles are right angles.

Rectangles are not polygons.

All sides of a rectangle are the same length.

The opposite sides of a rectangle are the same length.

In rectangles, one pair of opposite sides is parallel.

In rectangles, the diagonals cut each other in half.

All squares are rectangles, but not all rectangles are squares.

Rectangles are quadrilaterals.

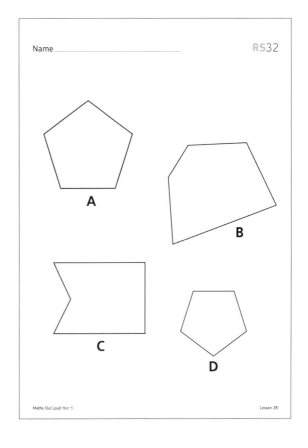

Name _____ RS32

A

B

C

D

Name _____

Pentagons

- How many diagonals do the shapes have?

- Do all five-sided shapes have the same number of diagonals?

- Are all diagonals the same length?

- How many triangles are there?

- What different kinds of triangle are there?

- What shapes are there apart from triangles?

Name _____

Critical evaluation

- Did you learn any new words today? Which ones?

- Will people be able to understand your shape profile?

- How many marks out of 10 would you give your shape profile for accuracy? Are the statements true?

- How many marks out of 10 would you give your shape profile for detail? Are there several statements?

- How many marks out of 10 would you give your shape profile for looks? Is it neat, clear and attractive?

- What would you do differently if you did the profile again?